Discovering Your Spiritual Portrait

Discovering Your Spiritual Portrait

Uncover Your Spiritual DNA

Mark Nysewander

Sovereign World

Sovereign World Ltd
PO Box 777
Tonbridge
Kent TN11 0ZS
England

Copyright © 2004 Mark Nysewander

All rights reserved. No part of this publication may be reproduced, stored in a retrieval system, or transmitted in any form or by any means, electronic, mechanical, photocopying or otherwise, without the prior written consent of the publisher. Short extracts may be used for review purposes.

All Scripture quotations are taken from the New International Version unless otherwise stated. Copyright © 1973, 1978 International Bible Society. Published by Hodder & Stoughton

ISBN 1 85240 377 2

The publishers aim to produce books which will help to extend and build up the Kingdom of God. We do not necessarily agree with every view expressed by the author, or with every interpretation of Scripture expressed. We expect each reader to make his/her judgment in the light of their own understanding of God's Word and in an attitude of Christian love and fellowship.

Cover design by CCD, www.ccdgroup.co.uk
Typeset by CRB Associates, Reepham, Norfolk
Printed in the United States of America

Contents

Introduction		7
PART 1: *The Gallery of Sinners*		9
Chapter 1	Reckless Sinners	10
Chapter 2	Decent Sinners	15
Chapter 3	Religious Sinners	20
Chapter 4	Forgiven Sinners	24
PART 2: *The Gallery of Believers*		29
Chapter 5	Ignorant Believers	30
Chapter 6	Selfish Believers	35
Chapter 7	Weary Believers	39
Chapter 8	Spirit-Filled Believers	44
PART 3: *The Gallery of Churches*		51
Chapter 9	Hardened Churches	52
Chapter 10	Wild Churches	57
Chapter 11	Renewed Churches	62

PART 4: *The Gallery of Disciples*   67

Chapter 12	Humble Disciples	68
Chapter 13	Submissive Disciples	73
Chapter 14	Tender Disciples	78
Chapter 15	Serving Disciples	83
	Conclusion	89
	Notes	91

Introduction

Finding Everyone's Portraits

Everyone's portrait is in this book. But don't look for your physical likeness. Look instead for your spiritual portrait.

Does that mean we all have a spiritual portrait? Yes. And our spiritual portraits are far more significant than the likeness of our physical features. The shape of your nose or the color of your eyes only has temporary concerns, but your spiritual DNA can be the reason for all kinds of present difficulties or blessings in your life. Your spiritual portrait even indicates your eternal destiny.

That's why all of us need to discover our spiritual portrait. Among the portraits in this book are many that show spiritual flaws. These flaws can create serious problems in your life. For that reason whenever you discover your portrait, you should ask, "Do I like what my spiritual condition is doing to my life?"

If you find some flaws in your appearance or in someone else's portrait, don't despair. Every one of these spiritual portraits can be changed! Although your physical features change little over the years, the wonderful truth about your spiritual DNA is that it can be transformed radically and instantly.

In fact, I write this book to encourage you, even if you have a flawed portrait. Why should you be encouraged? Because in this book you will not just encounter a portrait of how you look now. More importantly, you will discover a spiritual portrait of what you can become. When you find this portrait, realize that you can be transformed into what you are viewing.

What Should You Do?

If some of you find your spiritual DNA somewhat distressing, don't give up in frustration. Instead you should keep looking until you discover who you can become. The portrait of transformation will even show you how you can enter into this change.

Others of you have already experienced a major transformation in your spiritual condition. But you want more. Many of your features have been altered yet you need some final touches. You will find here the portrait of transformation that displays all those other changes you want for your life.

One more thing: study every portrait. Often you will not find your complete likeness in just one portrait. Your spiritual likeness can be a composite of several pictures. Only as you view all of these portraits will you discover all there is in you that can be changed.

Each of these portraits comes right out of Paul's letter to the Romans. In the beginning of his letter Paul identifies the power that can transform the spiritual appearances of people. He writes in Romans 1:16,

> "I am not ashamed of the gospel because it is the power of God for the salvation of everyone who believes."

Here's his point. Our spiritual transformation only comes through an outside power that he calls the gospel. So get ready. You are not only going to discover your spiritual portrait, but you are also about to encounter this gospel power that can change the way you look.

PART 1

The Gallery of Sinners

Our examination of spiritual portraits begins in the gallery of sinners. Sinners are people who miss what God wants for them because they reject His ways. That's what sin is, rejecting God's ways. And that's why every one of us is a sinner. In Romans 3:22–23 Paul makes it clear,

> *"There is no difference, for all have sinned and fall short of the glory of God."*

All means you and me.

Now our rejection of God and His ways damages our human spirit beyond repair. What is our human spirit? It is that fragile, unseen part of all of us, which touches the supernatural world. It is the only place where we can feel, hear and know God. Unfortunately, sin destroys the function of the human spirit. In this damaged condition there is no possibility of ever knowing God.

The first three portraits in the gallery of sinners portray different attempts to live with or deny that our human spirit is dead to God. Although all of us are sinners, we deal with our sinful condition in different ways. That's why there is more than one portrait. Everyone's likeness as a sinner is portrayed in one of these portraits.

You will also see a portrait of transformation. It shows the only way our human spirit can ever be restored to know the presence of God. Be sure you find this portrait of supernatural change. A human spirit dead to God can be transformed. All of us can know God's incredible presence today.

Chapter 1

Reckless Sinners

*"He gave them over to a depraved mind,
to do what ought not to be done."*
(Romans 1:28)

"I wandered farther away from you, and you let me go."[1]
(Augustine)

"A Harsh Bondage"

Look at this portrait and you see the face of pain. Reckless sinners live without any, or very few, restraints. Eventually their lifestyle leads them into pain. But it never starts out that way. They always begin with a reckless pursuit of pleasure.

In the early days of his life, Augustine certainly was not in pain. He was into pure pleasure. During his teens an uncontrolled desire for acceptance led Augustine to lie and steal. After leaving home to go off to school, he threw off more restraints and became sexually active with a young woman. Because of his reckless pursuit of pleasure, a baby was soon born. Augustine would trash hours of his time every week feeding a lust for entertainment. In a desperate search for meaning, he finally linked up to a cult that confused him and opened him up to demonic activity.

Then it happened, as it always does in the life of a reckless sinner. Pleasure is transformed into all kinds of inner pain. The pain became so great for Augustine that he tried to escape it by changing his ways. He sent away his girl friend, who he had lived with for 15 years. But he soon found himself in the arms of another women. Augustine said his painful addiction was a "harsh bondage".

Reckless sinners cast off all restraints just as Augustine did. Sooner or later though, their pursuit of pleasure without restraints becomes a free-fall toward pain.

Letting You Go

In Romans 1:24 Paul describes God's unusual response to reckless sinners. He says,

> *"Therefore God gave them over to the sinful desires of their hearts to sexual impurity for the degrading of their bodies with one another."*

What does Paul mean when he says that God gives reckless sinners over? Well, he isn't implying that God is through with them, or He has given up on them. Paul simply means that God gives reckless sinners over to sin. He gives them over because the greater their sin, the greater the pain.

You see, when the pain gets loud enough, it becomes a wake-up call for change. Since reckless sinners don't listen to God, maybe they will listen to their pain. Pain can be a very loud and persistent alarm. For that reason God refuses to do anything that will restrain their free-fall into pain. He gives them over to the sinful desires of their heart.

Now maybe you are thinking that it is very dangerous for God to give someone over to his or her sin. It is. For reckless sinners though, it would be much more dangerous if He didn't give them over. As sin increases so does the pain, until the pain is screaming at them to change direction. And then, just maybe, reckless sinners will respond to the scream.

Contamination

What are the signs of this attention-getting pain? Contamination is one sign. Their desire for forbidden supernatural experiences slowly pollutes reckless sinners with demonic activity. Or sexual freedom infects their bodies with irritating and even deadly diseases. Depression and uncontrollable upheavals of their psyches contaminate their emotions.

We all agree that contamination of any kind is alarming. It doesn't matter whether it is a stream of raw sewage seeping into a river, or columns of putrid smoke billowing into a clear sky. So reckless sinners may eventually become disgusted with the sludge of demonic activity, physical sickness and emotional disorder that their unrestrained desires dump into their lives. Whether it is a slow leak or a major spill, their reckless lifestyle is robbing them of a healthy body, clean spirit and clear mind.

Descent into the Abnormal

Not only is there a pain of contamination, there is also the pain of shame. A degraded lifestyle comes out of their reckless rebellion. Look at Paul's description of their lifestyle in Romans 1:28–29:

> "Furthermore, since they did not think it worthwhile to retain the knowledge of God, He gave them over to a depraved mind, to do what ought not to be done. They have become filled with every kind of wickedness, evil, greed and depravity."

When more and more abnormal activity starts to surface in their life, embarrassment and shame become their pain. But there is a way reckless sinners can temporarily relieve this pain. They can dull the pain by making these shameful actions seem normal.

Experiences they once considered unthinkable they now not only excuse, but also encourage all of us to accept. The shedding of innocent blood, the sexual abuse of men, women and children and the misuse of the human body are reinterpreted. Now more and more people are pressured to accept their reinterpretations as rights, entertainment and alternative lifestyles. If they don't put a spin on these experiences and don't convince everyone to accept these reinterpretations, then the shame would be unbearable for reckless sinners.

Degradation is disturbing. The only way reckless sinners can lessen their pain is to deny that it is degradation. Their greatest need is to honestly examine their lives and see if they live in denial.

Twisted Knots

Finally, there is the pain of bondage. In their freedom to expose their mind to whatever they desire, reckless sinners are no longer free to control their thoughts. Their freedom becomes bondage. Often it is demonic bondage. Romans 1:21 describes the mind of the reckless sinner when it says,

> *"For although they knew God, they neither glorified him as God nor gave thanks to him, but their thinking became futile and their foolish hearts were darkened."*

Remember the cruel bondage that came out of Nazi concentration camps in World War Two? German captors forced prisoners to work without enough food to give them strength. The torture in those camps from mental and physical experiments was beyond belief. Prisoners lived under a fear that paralyzed their life and destroyed all hope

As much as we abhor these stories of bondage, reckless sinners refuse to escape their own personal death camp. The forced labor to feed perverted habits and appetites of the mind is a daily demand in their lives. They are being subdued by the brainwashing techniques of demons. The regular torture of lust and jealousy breaks them down.

Augustine saw this same kind of bondage in his mind. Even though he was a brilliant student early in his life and later a gifted teacher, he was in pain. "The enemy had control of my will," he confessed, "and out of it he fashioned a chain and fettered me with it. For in truth lust is made out of a perverse will, and when lust is served, it becomes habit, and when habit is not resisted, it becomes necessity. By such links, joined one to another, as it were – a harsh bondage held me."[2]

His first 35 years were tangled up in a chain of addictions. God had given him over to his desires. Although his academic discipline was making him a good teacher, his bondage was keeping him in a constant state of personal pain. In looking at the effects of this rebellion Augustine once exclaimed, "Who can untie this most twisted and intricate mass of knots?"[3]

God gives reckless sinners over to their sinful desires. These desires become the pain of contamination, shame or bondage. Since they refuse to believe God, maybe they will believe their pain. If they don't then whatever pain is being experienced now in their life will continue to escalate and will absolutely consume them in the life to come.

Contamination, perversion and bondage portray the features of reckless sinners. If you recognize this as your portrait, God longs for you to wake up from your denial and escape your pain. He wants you to know that your portrait can be transformed!

Chapter 2

Decent Sinners

"Do you show contempt for the riches of his kindness, tolerance and patience, not realizing that God's kindness leads you toward repentance?"
(Romans 2:4)

"For I was a well-brought-up, right-thinking child of materialism. Beauty, I knew existed; but God, of course, did not."[4]
(Joy Davidman)

"Keeping God Out"

You will find very little pain in the portrait of these sinners. Here, just like reckless sinners, are people with spirits dead to the presence of God. Unlike the people in the first portrait these folks live decent and restrained lives.

Joy Davidman is a good example of a decent sinner. She was a Jew by birth and an atheist by choice. Her atheist parents lived a decent, moral life that came from their family tradition. Joy decided to throw out a lot of their morality and live for pleasure. But it wasn't a reckless pursuit of pleasure. "Lucky for me," she wrote, "my preferred pleasure happened to be reading, or I shouldn't have been able to stay out of hot water so well as I did. The only lasting damage my philosophy caused me was nearsightedness."[5]

Joy converted her life from pleasure to communism when she saw so many people with so many needs. She became deeply involved in the goals and inconsistencies of communism. But her commitment to communism began to fade when she married and became a mother. At that point, Joy's life and energy was given to her husband and sons.

As you can see, she was decent. There was no reckless sinning. As a young girl she was given over to pleasure but it never led to perversion. As a young woman she became a communist through the honorable goal of helping society. As a mother and wife she gave herself to her family. But Joy still had a rebellious heart. She said of God that "since childhood, I had been pouring half my energy into the task of keeping Him out."[6]

Decent sinners like Joy, have nothing degrading in their portrait. Their life is restrained, even moral. They may not believe in God, but they do believe in those things in which God believes. If anything leads to perversion, they avoid it. Decent sinners are wholesome and prosperous.

But don't be confused. They too have rejected God. His life does not dwell within their dead spirits. Yet, they desire what is good and God is keeping sin's destructive pain from them. He is seeking to bring decent sinners to Himself through His patience, not their pain.

This creates a bit of a problem. Decent sinners use all kinds of arguments based on their decency to deny that they are sinners. In reality, however, each of their arguments shows they have no excuse. In Romans 2:1 Paul speaks clearly to decent sinners when he says,

> "You therefore have no excuse, you who pass judgment on someone else, for at whatever point you judge the other, you are condemning yourself, because you who pass judgment do the same thing."

It Doesn't Look So Bad

Here is how they pass judgment on themselves when they judge others. Decent sinners look at reckless sinners and think, "I am not as bad as these people. I am not perverted or demonized. I am decent, therefore I must not be a sinner!"

They are only half-right. In comparison to reckless sinner,

their kind of rebellion is not perverted. Nevertheless it is still the same kind of rebellion found in reckless sinners. The rejection of God and a spirit dead to His presence are the evidence of rebellion. Decent sinners boast that the absence of outward perversion in their life means they are not sinners. It only means they are not that kind of sinner. And God, not them, is the reason that perversion is absent from their lives. His restraining power is working overtime through their conscience, training and culture to keep them from perversion. If God were to let up even for a moment, they would quickly slide into all kinds of degradation.

Joy was not perverted or addicted. But even she realized there was a side of her that could have erupted into reckless rebellion under the right circumstances. "By nature," she explained, "I am the sort of woman who nurses sick kittens and hates to spank her little boys; yet as a Marxist I would have been willing to shoot people without trial."[7]

Joy had no excuse and all other decent sinners don't either. Their inward rebellion may not manifest in outward perversion, but it is only because of God's restraining work. Paul asks decent sinners in Romans 2:4,

> *"Or do you show contempt for the riches of his kindness, tolerance and patience, not realizing that God's kindness leads you toward repentance?"*

Don't you see it? For decent sinners their life without perversion is a sign of God's kindness. It is meant to draw them to God.

It Doesn't Feel So Bad

Decent sinners sometimes think, "But I don't feel like a sinner. I'm not experiencing any pain because of my lifestyle. I don't feel the horrors and heartaches found in the first portrait. I have no sexually transmitted diseases. I'm not addicted to pornography. My life is good."

Yes, it is a pleasant life. But it is God who keeps it together. Using the restraining power of God as an argument that He is pleased with their rebellious heart is foolish. The absence of any pain in the lives of decent sinners is not evidence of their goodness. It is a tribute to God's patience over lives that continue to rebel against Him.

Even if they are not experiencing the pain of their rebellion on earth, it is no guarantee they will miss it in eternity. The Scriptures are clear when it declares in Romans 2:7-8,

> *"To those who by persistence in doing good seek glory, honor and immortality, he will give eternal life. But for those who are self seeking and reject the truth and follow evil, there will be wrath and anger."*

God receives those who seek *His* life, not a decent life. But for those who rebel against Him and do not have His life there is eternal pain. And it doesn't matter how decent they are now.

Here is the crucial question for decent sinners. Will they believe the Word of God or continue to count on their own decency? Since they don't feel pain, they may assume that their rebellion against God is of no great concern to Him. But none of us should mistake God's patience for His approval.

Pleading Ignorance

Again, decent sinners excuse themselves saying, "I'm not a very religious person. I don't really know any better. I'm ignorant of what God wants, so surely He will not hold my actions against me."

These folks may not know the details of God's requirements, but decent sinners know enough. There are other people with very little biblical knowledge and they know enough. They know they do wrong and God's life is not in them. They know they are in rebellion.

Decent sinners, if they are honest, know deep down that God's life is not within them and they are rebelling against Him. In their hearts there is enough evidence of rebellion against God to condemn them on the Day of Judgment. In Romans 2:9 Paul says,

> *"There will be trouble and distress for every human being who does evil: first for the Jew, then for the Gentile; but glory, honor*

and peace for everyone who does good: first for the Jew, then for the Gentile. For God does not show favoritism."

The greatest evil we can do is rebel against God and the greatest good is to have His life.

A Locked-In Response

Once in a trial, the defendant standing before the judge was asked if he swore to tell the whole truth and nothing but the truth? The defendant responded with a stone face, "I do not."

A day is coming when all of us will stand before the Judge. It will not matter how decent our life was, how good we feel, or how little we understand. Our heart will then be paralyzed with a fixed response. The capacity to change ceases at death. God will ask, "Do you want to come and live with me forever?" From the secrets of a rebellious heart that is void of His presence, decent sinners will answer emphatically, with all the demons of hell, "I do not!"

Perhaps you see this as your portrait. As a decent sinner under God's patience, you claim that the absence of perversion in your portrait means you are not a sinner. It only means that you are not that kind of sinner. Is it worth gambling away your life on such an excuse?

Chapter 3

Religious Sinners

"... you then who teach others, do you not teach yourself?"
(Romans 2:21)

"... I, who went to America to convert others, was never myself converted to God."[8]
(John Wesley)

~~~~

"Saving My Own Soul"

The strong feature of this portrait is not pain or even decency, but *religion*. The people portrayed here are still sinners but they are religious sinners. Now maybe you're wondering how someone can be religious and at the same time a sinner. It is simple. Many sinners desperately try to fill the absence of God's presence in their empty spirits with religion. They become sinners who are religious. John Wesley was one of these religious sinners.

Here is how he combined religion and rebellion. He packed his days with religion hoping it would change him. When he went off to school to prepare for the ministry, he organized some of his fellow students into a group to keep a set of intricate rules and regulations. John himself, would get up at 4:00 a.m. to begin his day with prayer, reading, service, worship and devotion. He consumed books that spoke of obtaining a holy life. When he completed school instead of becoming the pastor of a church, John decided to be a missionary to a foreign country. This action, like all else he had been doing, was to fill his empty spirit. He wrote a friend, "My chief motive, to which all the rest are subordinate is the hope of saving my own soul." But John became disappointed in his missionary experience. It didn't save his soul.

At 35 years of age John had built a tower of religion to reach God. He capped it off by becoming a missionary. But all these rules, sacrifices and laws had not brought him to God. On his journey home from the unsuccessful missionary endeavor he cried from out of his dead spirit, "Oh, who shall convert me?"[9]

Don't let John's religion fool you. He is simply a sinner in a religious environment. It matters little whether rebellion is in the saloon or in the sanctuary; it still separates our human spirit from God.

Religious sinners like John, carry some very dangerous presumptions. We all need to be careful! It is possible to live, grow up and die in a religious environment and still miss God altogether. It happens when we presume that certain religious activities mean we are not sinners.

Full of Knowledge

Religious sinners presume that the learning and teaching of religious knowledge means they are not sinners. It doesn't mean any such thing. They can quote the Bible, know God's will and attend church but still rebel against God. Romans 2:18–21 is a description of religious sinners. It says you can be a sinner even,

> "... if you know his will and approve what is superior because you are instructed by the law, if you are convinced you are a guide for the blind, a light for those who are in the dark, an instructor of the foolish, a teacher of infants, because you have in the law the embodiment of knowledge and truth."

It is possible religious sinners have even raised children to do what is superior, and all their children have become religious like them. But if they have a heart void of the presence of God and full of rebellion against Him, there is no basic difference between religious sinners and reckless sinners.

Yes, religious sinners may be making a better contribution to society, but like reckless sinners they aren't making any contribution to eternity!

If religious knowledge could give us God's presence then the people with the most knowledge would be saints. However, there are people who know the Bible thoroughly, yet they are empty of divine life. It would also mean that people ignorant of religious information would be the most helpless sinners. Again, there are people who cannot read or write, but they glow with the very presence of God.

It does not matter how much of the Scriptures religious sinners can quote or how many religious truths they have learned. When their heart is full of rebellion and dead to God's presence, then they are no more than sinners with impressive religious knowledge.

Virtual Reality

Because religious sinners participate in religious activity, they think they are experiencing God. The activity may be circumcision, baptism, worship, confession, or first communion. Somehow they assume that going through such rituals signifies they are no longer sinners. Paul warns us in Romans 2:25 that religious activity doesn't always have value. Speaking of the religious ritual of circumcision, he says,

> *"Circumcision has value if you observe the law, but if you break the law you have become as though you had not been circumcised."*

And as we already discovered, in our rebellion we all have broken the law.

It is not outward activity but inward reality that gives the ritual its value! A ritual is an outward expression of an inward experience. Our participation in an outward ritual does not guarantee we are experiencing any spiritual reality. Outward circumcision does not automatically mean there is a spiritual circumcision of the heart. Water baptism is no guarantee we have been immersed into the presence of God. These are rituals but they are not always realities. Unless we are experiencing God, all these activities and rituals have no value. They can't bring God to our dead spirit. Ritual can only be a blessing because He has already come.

Doing Enough

Here's another presumption. Religious sinners presume that the observance of religious rules and regulations means they are not sinners. They think that if disobeying God makes them sinners, then obeying God's laws, long enough and well enough, will surely make them OK again.

This was John Wesley's plan. "By my continued endeavor to keep His whole law, inward and outward, to the utmost of my power," John wrote, "I was persuaded that I should be accepted of Him."[10] Again, John's tower of religious laws fell short of God's presence.

God's forgiveness for rebellion and His life are not received by obeying religious laws. God gives his law as a protection, a restraint, and as a moral model. Most importantly, the law shows that we are impotent to transform our spiritual portrait by human effort. Romans 3:20 announces to all of us,

> *"Therefore no one will be declared righteous in his sight by observing the law, rather, through the law we become conscious of sin."*

Why does God do such a thing? Why does He give a law that cannot free us from the effects of our rebellion? Is this some kind of cosmic joke like pulling wings off butterflies? No! God gave the law to point out the solution to our problem. The answer to the problem of sin will never be found in our efforts to be good, but only in God's power. The law is a sober reminder. It is not within us to bring life back to our dead spirit.

Are you a religious sinner? You are if you presume your religious knowledge, ritual and observance means God dwells in you. But how can He be in you when your spirit is still dead to him? It is possible your religious activities are no more than a religious cover for a rebellious heart and dead spirit without God's presence.

Chapter 4

Forgiven Sinners

"... We have peace with God through our Lord Jesus Christ."
(Romans 5:1)

"Instantly ... all the dark shadows of doubt fled away."[11]
(Augustine)

"All my defenses ... went down momentarily. And God came in."[12]
(Joy Davidman)

"About a quarter before nine ... I felt my heart strangely warmed."[13]
(John Wesley)

A Portrait of Life

Observe here a radically different portrait from the previous three. This is the portrait of transformation. The persons portrayed in this portrait no longer display the characteristics of sinners. Rebellion is gone. They have peace with God. Their human spirits, once riddled with sin and dead to divine life, are now on fire with God's presence. The source of their greatest fulfillment is God, and the hope of enjoying Him forever. This is the portrait of forgiven sinners.

This kind of transformation comes to us through faith. Forgiven sinners are believers. Here is what they believe.

First, the Bad News

They believe the bad news. When God says everyone has sinned, forgiven sinners understand that none of us are exempt. Romans 3:10–12 declares,

> *"There is no one righteous, not even one; there is no one who understands, no one who seeks God. All have turned away, they have together become worthless; there is no one who does good, not even one."*

Reckless sinners listen to their pain and admit they are in bondage to Satan. Decent sinners put aside their excuses and confess they are in rebellion against God. Religious sinners abandon their presumptions and accept the fact they have sinned.

Forgiven sinners don't just believe the bad news that they are sinners, they believe the worst of the bad news. The worst of the bad news says that there is nothing any of us can do to change our condition as sinners. You can change from being a reckless sinner to decent one, or from a decent sinner to a religious one – but you will still be a sinner! We cannot take away the disease of our rebellion nor put the life of God into our dead spirits. Romans 3:20 is crystal clear when it says,

> *"Therefore no one will be declared righteous in his sight by observing the law; rather, through the law we become conscious of sin."*

Remember reckless Augustine? He began to recognize this bad news that he was a sinner. It was through the prayers of a loving mother and the sermons of a gifted preacher. He made several attempts at reforming his life only to realize he could not bring divine life and forgiveness to his dead spirit.

In the depths of despair, while in a private garden, he sought the Lord for help. It was then that he heard a voice chanting, "Take up and read, take up and read." Augustine interpreted it as a command from God. He picked up the New Testament and it opened to Romans 13:14. The first words he saw were "Clothe yourself with the Lord Jesus Christ and do not think about how to gratify desires of the sinful nature." Augustine turned from his old life and believed for this covering of Jesus. Immediately and completely the hand of God emptied a pit of corruption out from his dead spirit. He was forgiven!

Now, the Good News

Forgiven sinners believe the bad news that says there is absolutely nothing we can do to change our sinful lives. But the good news as Augustine and every other forgiven sinner discovers is that the solution for our spiritual condition is not found in what we can do for God, but rather in what God can do for us. Paul says in Romans 3:21,

> *"But now a righteousness from God, apart from the law, has been made known, to which the Law and the Prophets testify."*

In other words, God apart from our human efforts is able to forgive our rebellion and bring divine life to our dead spirits. Transformation comes from God, not from us. The power of God changes forgiven sinners just like Augustine.

There is more. Forgiven sinners don't just believe the good news. They believe the best of the good news: God's transforming power comes to us through a relationship with His Son, Jesus Christ. Paul explains in Romans 3:22,

> *"This righteousness from God comes through Jesus Christ to all who believe."*

The good news is that God can transform our portrait. The best news is that He does it through someone who will become our greatest joy and friend.

Some folks think it is religious bigotry to say that Jesus Christ is the best of all religions. This is not the claim! Jesus Christ is not a religion. A religion is a system wherein people do things for God. Jesus Christ is a person through whom God does something for us. God has chosen Jesus as the sole means of bringing our dead spirits back to life. Jesus Christ is God's only begotten Son. He alone has paid the penalty for everyone's rebellion by His death upon the cross. Only Jesus Christ has been raised from the dead triumphing over Satan's power. He is the living Lord who can put the life of God into our spirits. Jesus Christ is not a religion; He is good news.

Remember decent Joy Davidman. She wanted absolutely nothing to do with Jesus Christ. "As a Jew," she explained, "I had been led to feel cold chills at the mention of His name. Is this strange? For a thousand years Jews have lived among people who interpret Christ's will to mean floggings and burnings, 'gentleman's agreements' and closed universities."[14]

A day came when Joy was completely helpless, and her life was out of control. In that moment she got on her knees and prayed. Suddenly she met God. It lasted about half a minute, but what she tasted, she wanted. She began to study religions to find out who was this God she had encountered. "And the Redeemer who had made Himself known," she concluded, "whose personality I would recognize among ten thousand – well, when I read the New Testament, I recognized Him. He was Jesus."[15]

Getting in Touch with Jesus

Forgiven sinners believe the bad news and then, like Joy, they believe the good news. Finally, they believe in Jesus Christ. By faith they make contact with the living presence of Jesus Christ.

How do you believe into Jesus Christ? First, believe He is present, aggressively pursuing you to rescue you from Satan's bondage and to forgive your sins. Second, admit the bad news to Him that you are a sinner dead in your spirit and rebelling against God. Now, confess to Him any and every sin that comes to your mind. In the name and by the authority of Jesus Christ receive the forgiveness of your sins and ask Jesus to give you the life of His Father. Finally, believe what Jesus is doing in you and choose to follow Him daily.

The evidence of His forgiveness and His gift of new life come to us in different ways. For some it is like an explosion of love. The guilt of sin immediately disappears. Their human spirit comes alive with joy, and they sense the presence of

Jesus Christ surging into their life. For others there is no great sensation. They just accept that Jesus Christ is doing what He says He will do. Over the days and weeks a sense of His presence and peace begins to surface in their life. The feelings will come and go, but the deep spiritual experience of Jesus Christ's forgiveness will remain. God has done an awesome work in the hearts of forgiven sinners through Jesus Christ. Romans 5:5 tells us,

> *"And hope does not disappoint us, because God has poured out his love into our hearts by the Holy Spirit, which he has given us."*

In John Wesley, the religious sinner, forgiveness came with a sense of spiritual fire. When John went to and returned from the mission field he met with a group of lively believers who encouraged him to put his faith in Jesus Christ. Back home he attended a Bible study where faith was explained. As he listened, John believed in Jesus. It was then he felt a strange warmth of divine life come to his heart. But just as important as the inward sense of eternal life was the deep experience of forgiveness. "I felt I did trust Christ, Christ alone for salvation;" he wrote, "And an assurance was given me that He had taken away my sins, even mine, and saved me from the law of sin and death."[16]

Here is the beautiful portrait of transformation that God has placed in the gallery of sinners. Its beauty is found in the peace and joy that is portrayed. But it is also beautiful because all of us, just like Augustine, Joy Davidman and John Wesley, can be transformed into this likeness. To you and everyone else, God whispers, "I can make you like this through my Son, Jesus Christ."

PART 2

The Gallery of Believers

We now leave the gallery of sinners and turn to examine four portraits in a different gallery. You won't find any more portraits of sinners here. Instead all the portraits in this gallery are of believers. They believe Jesus Christ for the forgiveness of their sins and they trust God for his life to come into their dead spirits.

Although none of these portray sinners, some of the portraits still feature spiritual flaws. Even when the initial transformation of forgiveness comes, many of us are still weak believers. We are not experiencing the full transformation that God intends for everyone.

As was true previously, in this section you are going to find another three portraits. These are of weak believers. Each one portrays a different kind of weakness and how we attempt to deal it.

Beside the portraits of weak believers there is also another portrait of transformation. This unique portrait portrays God's strength for all of us. Paul speaks of the incredible energy of God that is available to everyone who is weak. In Romans 8:26 he says,

> "In the same way, the Spirit helps us in our weakness."

The final portrait shows you how we can be filled with the Holy Spirit.

This is the portrait of transformation in the gallery of believers. Through it you will discover the promise of God's power for all of us who believe.

Chapter 5

Ignorant Believers

"We died to sin; how can we live in it any longer?"
(Romans 6:2)

"Divine love drew me gently and sweetly in one direction, while natural vanity violently dragged me in another."[17]
(Jeanne Marie Guyon)

"Some Secret Motive"

The believers you will examine in this portrait are flawed by the spiritual weakness of ignorance. Here is how it happens. When God's life enters into an empty spirit through the forgiveness of Jesus Christ; there is immediate satisfaction and joy. But it doesn't take long before many believers discover a weakness in their new life. They find a desire to live for God but an inability to do it. This weakness many times leads to sin. Their weakness comes through ignorance. These believers are ignorant of all that God can do in us.

Jeanne Guyon had this flaw of ignorance. She believed Jesus to forgive her at the age of twenty. She was a very attractive woman whose interest had once been drawn completely to her own pleasure. She never was a reckless sinner, but she was a decent person consumed by her own selfish enjoyment and pride. Immediately after her conversion from a sinner to a believer she concentrated on keeping these selfish appetites under control. But they kept erupting up into her life.

"In my conversations with others," she wrote, "I could often discover some secret motive which was evil."[18] Jeanne saw in her daily experiences as a believer a strong impulse toward sin.

She hungered for a freedom from this pull toward sin. It was during this period she met a man who described her condition and her need. He helped her understand that God wants more in us than a heart that is just forgiven. God can give us a heart that is holy.

Like Jeanne, ignorant believers have forgiven hearts but they don't have changed hearts. They aren't holy. They believe Jesus forgives them, but they are not aware He can change them. Their lives as believers, therefore, slip into continual sin.

Ignorant believers do not display God's best. God's work in the human heart does not climax with a life of habitual sin. There is so much more. His intention is to manifest through us the life and character of His Son. God is committed to make us holy, like Jesus.

So, why do ignorant believers still sin? It is simple. Although they believe Jesus Christ for His forgiveness and divine life, they still don't understand all that Jesus wants to do in their lives. Look at what they already believe, and then look at how much more they need to believe.

Incomplete Faith in What Jesus Has Done

Ignorant believers trust for only some of the benefits of Jesus' death. But they must believe for all that Jesus did on the cross. Jesus Christ not only died to forgive us; He died to deliver us. There is more good news to believe than what these people already believe.

Because of what Jesus did on the cross, a life of habitual sin is not necessary. Paul writes in Romans 6:6–7,

> *"For we know that our old self was crucified with him so that the body of sin might be done away with, that we should no longer be slaves to sin – because anyone who has died has been freed from sin."*

Our twist toward sinning can be straightened. Jesus Christ breaks the power of sin!

This doesn't mean we will no longer be tempted. We can still mess up because of the dysfunctions in our lives and our ignorance of God's will. But through the cross you and I can receive enough divine power to resist intentional sin, overcome our dysfunctions and grow in the knowledge of God's purposes.

If believers don't know this truth of deliverance, what's their alternative? They will habitually sin. They will live as though Jesus Christ's death does not meet all their needs. They will think He can forgive them, but He can't liberate them from the gravitational pull of sin. There is more to the power of Jesus Christ than this kind of life! What Jesus did on the cross blossoms into something greater than a life of habitual sinning. Jesus Christ not only brings forgiveness, He brings deliverance.

Consider this. If ignorant believers know there is enough power in the blood of Jesus Christ to help them resist sin for a moment, then why do they not know there is enough power to help them consistently resist sin for a minute, a day, a week or a year? They will never live above sin until they know that Jesus has made it possible to do so. Romans 6:11–12 reads,

> *"In the same way, count yourself dead to sin but alive to God in Christ Jesus. Therefore do not let sin reign in your mortal body so that you obey its evil desires."*

Only when we add up everything Jesus had done for us by faith will we be dead to sin through the cross of Jesus.

Incomplete Faith in What The Spirit Is Doing

There's more. Ignorant believers must also understand everything the Spirit can do within them. When they believed in Jesus, God's life came into them in the person of the Holy Spirit. Think of it, they have dwelling within them the same power that raised Jesus from the dead!

This Holy Spirit who imparts into us the benefits of Jesus' death upon the cross, is very powerful. He can change our desires so we choose what Jesus would choose. He can change our thoughts so we think as Jesus thinks. He can change our emotions so that we feel as Jesus feels. Speaking of the work of the Holy Spirit in believers, Paul says in Romans 6:4,

> *"Just as Christ was raised from the dead through the glory of the Father, we too may live a new life."*

The Holy Spirit has the power to manifest in us a new life, the very character of Jesus Christ. If He is that powerful, why are ignorant believers not seeing these changes in their lives? Because the Holy Spirit only changes what we yield to Him. When we believe in Jesus, the Holy Spirit establishes residence in our human spirit. Now, we must invite Him to fill other areas of our lives, like our mind, will and emotions. As we yield, the Holy Spirit releases more of His power to transform each area of our life. Although every believer has the Holy Spirit, not every believer is *filled* with the Holy Spirit.

Paul speaks of the importance of yielding to the Holy Spirit in Romans 6:13. He says,

> *"Do not offer the parts of your body to sin, as instruments of wickedness, but rather offer yourself to God, as those who have been brought from death to life and offer the parts of your body to him as instruments of righteousness."*

Ignorant believers are not going to yield their lives to the Holy Spirit until they believe He has the power to change the way they think, choose and feel. Without such faith, their only future is one of habitually sinning.

Ignorant of this truth, believers will live as though the Holy Spirit, through whom God created the world and raised Jesus from the dead, is unable to change their hearts. But look – as believers the life of God dwells within us! His power is greater than any of our sinful habits and patterns.

Complete Your Faith

It is true. Ignorant believers trust that through Jesus' death on the cross their sins are forgiven. But now they must believe more – they must believe that through the cross they can be delivered from the power of sin.

Yes, they believe the Holy Spirit has established a beachhead in their human spirits. Now they must go even further. Ignorant believers should invite the same Holy Spirit to launch an all out invasion of power throughout their lives.

God provides the power to break the gravitational pull of sin by the cross. He also gives the power to become like Jesus through the Holy Spirit. Faith releases the blessings of God's power. If you are an ignorant believer, please understand it will never happen until you first *know* it can happen. The only other alternative as an ignorant believer is a life of habitual sinning.

Chapter 6

Selfish Believers

"... you are slaves to the one whom you obey."
(Romans 6:16)

"I saw the humility of Jesus, and my pride ..."[19]
(Samuel Brengle)

"Making a Name for Myself"

Here is another portrait of weak believers. As you will discover, the main feature in this portrait is not ignorance. It is selfishness. As we saw in the last portrait, some believers don't believe enough because they don't know any better. But other believers don't believe enough because they just don't want to. In their self-interest they choose to be weak. This is the portrait of a selfish believer.

Look at Sam Brengle's portrait for a good view of a selfish believer. He tried to juggle his selfish ambition and Jesus' forgiveness at the same time. He believed in Jesus as a young boy. Through his years in school he developed as a gifted speaker. Soon young Sam saw this as a way of making a name for himself. He spent hours in study and sought opportunities to speak. At first he determined to exercise his gifted speech in the profession of law, which would be his avenue to fame.

While he pursued law, he kept hearing the Lord call him to preach. He tried to stifle the voice of God that would wreck his selfish plan for fame. In a moment of desperation however,

Sam promised God he would preach if God would answer a prayer. It wasn't good for Sam to try and cut a deal with God, because the Lord answered his prayer. Sam had to accept God's call into ministry.

So he poured himself into being a preacher. He would still fulfill his selfish desire of being a great speaker, but he would now do it behind the pulpit instead of before the bench. He was still obsessed with his plan.

Sam's is the portrait of selfish faith. Look at the implications of the actions of selfish believers. These actions are not normal. While warmly accepting Jesus' forgiveness selfish believers are, like Sam, resisting the Holy Spirit's deliverance from their self-interest.

Insulting Jesus

Most normal believers understand they are forgiven of their sins in order to obey Jesus Christ. They are forgiven so they can give total devotion to Jesus as Lord.

Selfish faith however, is abnormal. Although they are saved from sin's guilt and Satan's bondage, selfish believers feel it is too much of a hassle to obey Jesus. Because of what they want to do, Jesus can wait. They abort God's purpose in their lives in order to continue as their own master. These believers reason, "Can't I do what I want to do since I am forgiven? Why should I be a fanatic?"

Paul anticipates their question and he has an answer for them when he writes in Romans 6:15,

> *"Shall we sin because we are not under the law but under grace? By no means!"*

Why is Paul so strong in his answer? Because selfish believers have an attitude that is the height of arrogance. It is an insult to the Lord Jesus Christ. They are taking the blessings of Jesus' death, but refusing Jesus Himself. They are using His sacrifice to salve their conscience in order to continue in their self-indulgence.

It's not only an insult, it is very dangerous! Such selfish disobedience has the potential of vandalizing the work of

God beyond recognition in the lives of these believers. As a believer, we are only safe when we are in obedience to Jesus as Lord and friend.

Insulting Self

Again normal believers rejoice that they are delivered from an impure lifestyle so they can have a lifestyle like Jesus Christ's. God has forgiven us in order to fill us with His Holy Spirit. God is absolutely committed to producing the character of His Son in the believer's life. This is our destiny and we should want it!

Selfish believers, on the other hand, resist the fullness of the Holy Spirit. Occasional sins, forbidden desires and personal ambitions are far more important to them than living like Jesus. In Romans 6:19 Paul calls these believers to move beyond this kind of selfish living. He says,

> *"Just as you used to offer the parts of your body in slavery to impurity and to ever increasing wickedness, so now offer them in slavery to righteousness leading to holiness."*

As they compromise their salvation because of self-interest, they insult themselves!

When Sam was in seminary, he heard about the baptism of the Holy Spirit that would deliver him from his selfish ambition. As he sought the Lord for this work, he was shocked at how full he was of self-interest. "I got my eyes off everybody but Jesus and myself," he said, "and I came to loathe myself."[20]

Selfish believers need to see like Sam that their selfish faith is an insult to themselves! As a selfish believer, they are robbing themselves of knowing the life for which they are made. Refusing the Holy Spirit's power to completely transform our lives is to trash our spiritual destinies.

Insulting Others

Finally, normal believers no longer transmit the bad effect of their sin to others. Instead they now minister the blessings of Jesus Christ to people. Once they spread sin and brokenness to those around them. Now they blossom with the works of the Holy Spirit.

Selfish believers too, have been delivered from spreading the fall-out of a sinful life. As selfish believers however, they refuse to enter into the ministry of the Holy Spirit and spread the overflow of an anointed life. In Romans 7:6, Paul describes the life they should seek. He says,

> "But now by dying to what once bound us, we have been released from the law so that we serve in the new way of the Spirit and not in the old way of the written code."

These believers however, devote their energies to their own selfish agenda rather than serving in the manifestation of the Spirit's power. They don't want to be bothered with doing the ministry of Jesus.

This is an insult to the people who live around them. Selfish believers receive divine life from Jesus, but only give out selfish actions. Friends, family and a desperate world are seeking what they have found in Jesus Christ. By indulging in their own pleasures they are excluding these people from the blessings of God.

Our privilege as believers is to extend the life we have received in Jesus Christ to the people around us. To accept these blessings and refuse to pass them on is to block the work of God in this world!

A life that does not seek for the manifestation of Jesus' character and ministry is a terrible disservice. If you are a selfish believer you insult Jesus, hurt yourself, and cheat others of the truth you have experienced. Repent of your selfishness because it robs you of what God wants to do. Your destiny is to enter completely into the fullness of God. Selfish believer, exchange your selfish lifestyle for the fullness of the Holy Spirit.

Chapter 7

Weary Believers

"I have the desire to do what is good, but I can not carry it out."
(Romans 7:18)

"We prayed for strength, and no strength came."[21]
(Agnes Sanford)

❦ ❦

"Always and Incessantly Tired"

Weariness is the main characteristic of this portrait. Unlike ignorant believers the believers portrayed in this portrait understand and desire everything that God says is possible for them. And unlike selfish believers these folks are going after the full life of God. But here is their weakness: they go after the full life of God in their own strength. Eventually it wears them completely out.

Agnes Sandford had the weaknesses of weary believers. Here is a glimpse of her portrait. At the age of nine Agnes came to Jesus. She grew up in a missionary home where her Dad was orthodox but Agnes stated, "The Holy Spirit worked through him yet not quite in him." Later on, as a young adult, Agnes worried about people coming to Jesus but soon slipping away. "Only the Holy Ghost, the Sanctifier," she explained, "can keep us in the love of Jesus and protect us from the anger and bitterness of this world and bring us into the glory of the sons of God." Then she confessed, "And we did not know the Holy Spirit or have His power."[22]

After Agnes married and had children she started wrestling with deep depression. She sought help from a minister who believed in the healing power of Jesus. It was from his ministry and some earlier experiences in prayer that she started to pray for the sick. Through her prayers people were healed and she became more and more acquainted with the Holy Spirit. Yet much of her ministry was a weary effort that exhausted her. "For many years," Agnes wrote, "while I did the works of prayer and healing in Jesus' name, the Holy Spirit was obliged to push His way, as it were, through all the burdens and fears of this world. I did not know then that the outburst of power called the baptism in the Spirit was available just as it was on the day of Pentecost, and so I had not received the infilling of power that awakens within one the well-spring of life."[23]

The healing power of Jesus continued to flow through Agnes, but her ever-increasing ministry, busy home-life and writing could no longer be carried by her strength. "I was always and increasingly tired," she remembered

Unlike the selfish believer, Agnes desperately wanted the life of Jesus reproduced in her. Unfortunately, she was trying to get it without the Spirit of God. She believed God could forgive her but after that she took over. Like Agnes, it is by human effort that weary believers are striving for the full life of Jesus Christ.

Look at how they live their spiritual life. At first glance, these activities seem to be noble. On closer examination however, they really indicate that weary believers do not fully believe.

Living by the Rules

Weary believers try to produce the character of Jesus in their lives by laws. They measure the depth of their spiritual lives by codes, rules, and a string of do's and don'ts. The more of these they master, the more they perceive themselves as living like Jesus. Regulations fill their lives.

But God has not forgiven us so He can fill our lives with rules. He has forgiven us so He can fill us with the Holy Spirit. The depth of our spiritual lives are not measured by how many codes we keep.

This does not mean that rules and regulations are wrong. They are just inadequate to make believers like Jesus and to fight against the continuous pull of Satan.

If you ever learn a new language, you discover that a constant exposure to someone who speaks that language is the best way to learn it. Rules can help you understand the grammar of the language, but they are inadequate to teach you how to speak fluently. In the same way, as believers we will never learn to live the life of Jesus by rules. His life is beyond our ability to learn. The only way to manifest the life of Jesus is by full exposure to Him through the infilling of the Holy Spirit.

Codes and laws don't make believers like Jesus, but the Holy Spirit does. He can move us deeper into Jesus' nature. We have been released from fulfilling the law by human effort in order to fulfill God's will through His Spirit.

When we were sinners we could never obey enough rules to bring forgiveness to our dead spirits. Now, as believers we will never obey enough regulations to bring Jesus' character to our lives. Weary believers try. But they wear themselves out attempting to do something that human effort cannot accomplish. Paul himself testified in Romans 7:10,

"I found that the very commandment that was intended to bring life actually brought death."

Activity of Receptivity

Weary believers also attempt to produce the ministry of Jesus in their lives by human activity. Since becoming believers they want to show their gratitude to God for what He had done in them, so they fill their lives with religious activity. The more they do, the more they assume it will please God and make them like Jesus.

But they did not become believers by human activity. How then, do they expect to grow as believers by such activity? The life of a believer is a miracle. It begins by the activity of God. His power maintains it. And when completed, it will only be God's work.

Weary believers should not measure their progress as believers by the amount of human activity they squeeze into their lives. They should measure it by the amount of divine activity that overflows their lives. God is not looking for religious activity; rather He is looking for receptivity to His power. Believers are called to exercise faith in God and surrender every area of their lives to God's Spirit.

Human activity has no more strength to deliver us from sin than it did to forgive us of sin. It has no more power to fill us with the Spirit of God than it does to give us the same Holy Spirit. Again, Paul explains in Romans 7:18-19,

> "For I have the desire to do what is good but I cannot carry it out. For what I do is not the good I want to do; no, the evil I do not want to do – this I keep doing."

Attempting to grow by human activity is to get on a never-ending treadmill.

Burnout

The strongest evidence that people are weary believers is exhaustion from their hard labor. Have you seen those shocking photos of people confined in concentration camps? Their faces are hollow, depressed and dark. That is the look of exhaustion from hard labor without relief. They were given work that could never be completed and barely enough food to stay alive.

That is also the portrait of weary believers. Their spirits are exhausted and depressed. They burn themselves out attempting to be like Jesus through human effort. Their lives are spiritual experiences of hard labor. From their hearts they scream Paul's words. In Romans 7:24 he cries,

> "What a wretched man I am! Who will rescue me from the body of death?"

The grind of trying to keep laws and do God's work by their strength is tiresome. All such labor culminates in exhaustion. It's commendable that weary believers want everything that God wants for them – but they can't make it happen through hard labor. Eventually they will tire of trying.

Weary believers have good intentions because they want to be like Jesus. But, they are attempting to fulfill those intentions with rules and activities. All their good intentions, regulations and activities will not produce the character and ministry of Jesus in their hearts. Only God can do that.

He does it through His Holy Spirit. God is not looking for our good intentions; He is looking for our faith. He is not looking for human effort to fulfill laws; rather He wants us filled full of the Spirit. He is not seeking our activity, but His activity through our believing heart. If this is your portrait, repent of your attempts to make yourself what God wants to make you. Let Him deliver you from your unending work. Escape your hard labor camp and come into the freedom of His Spirit.

Chapter 8

Spirit-Filled Believers

"... Those who live in accordance with the Spirit have their minds set on what the Spirit desires."
(Romans 8:5)

"Every ambition for self was now gone."[24]
(Sam Brengle)

"Everything that I did either with the mind or the body, could now be done with about half the energy it once required and in about half the time."[25]
(Agnes Sanford)

"Doing good was now my nature."[26]
(Jeanne Guyon)

Emptied and Filled

Viewing the last three portraits you discovered that God has not forgiven ignorant believers so they can sin habitually. And He hasn't given selfish believers His divine presence so they can live a selfish life. Nor has He done these things so weary believers can be religious by their own human effort. God really wants to deliver all believers from the power of sin and self. He desires to fill us with the Holy Spirit. This is the portrait of transformation in the gallery of believers. Spirit-filled believers trust God for all that He wants to do in them through His Holy Spirit.

The Spirit-filled life is both an emptying and a filling. Spirit-filled believers empty each area of their lives to make room for the Holy Spirit, who has been confined in their human spirit. Then they invite the Holy Spirit to fill all these area of their lives. They are emptied through surrender and filled through faith. That's how it happens. Look at the areas that need to be emptied and filled.

Filling Your Mind

When the Holy Spirit fills believers, He enters and transforms their minds with the thoughts of Jesus. Whereas their minds were once preoccupied with their agendas, they now become preoccupied with God's agenda. Romans 8:6 reads,

> *"The mind of sinful man is death, but the mind controlled by the Spirit is life and peace; the sinful mind is hostile to God."*

When Sam the selfish believer, discovered how his mind was filled with a selfish agenda hostile to God's purposes, it caused him great concern. He soon was hungry for the sanctifying work of the Spirit. He said, "I was willing to appear a big blunder and a complete failure if only He would cleanse me and dwell in me!"[27] He emptied his mind of his ambition and reputation in complete self-renunciation.

In a quiet act of faith Sam believed God to fill him with the Holy Spirit. Although he experienced no great sensation of the Spirit in that moment, two mornings later God manifest His presence in a baptism of love. "I walked out over Boston Commons before breakfast, weeping for joy and praising God. Oh how I loved! In that hour I knew Jesus, and I loved Him till it seemed my heart would break with love."[28] Sam's mind was now flowing with the "life and peace" of Jesus.

If we ask for the fullness of the Holy Spirit and refuse any of His influence on our minds then we are not really seeking for His fullness. The baptism of the Holy Spirit is not a good case of goose bumps! It is receiving the very mind of Jesus Christ.

The Holy Spirit cannot fill something already cluttered. As with Sam, He will prompt believers to give up their present preoccupations. If the minds of Spirit-filled believers are concerned for their reputation, He may call them to become fools for Jesus. If they are worried about personal comforts, He could call them to some acts of sacrifice. If they are filled with pride, He may call them to obscure service. He will empty them of their self-preoccupations.

Then by faith the Spirit fills their minds with Jesus' preoccupations. As Spirit-filled believers they begin to seek the glory of God and desire fellowship with the Father. Ways to bring a lost world to Jesus Christ will surface in their minds. As they expose their minds to the Holy Spirit's revelations, they will become saturated with the thoughts of Jesus. These thoughts become the great vision for their lives.

Strengthening Your Body

But the Holy Spirit not only transforms minds; He also fills the bodies of Spirit-filled believers with a new power to do the work of God. In Romans 8:11 we have a clear promise. It says,

> *"And if the Spirit of him who raised Jesus from the dead is living in you, he who raised Christ from the dead will also give life to your mortal bodies through his Spirit, who lives in you."*

Imagine it. The same power that raised Jesus from the dead can flow through us. As the Holy Spirit fills, we are infused with energy beyond our own.

Remember the weary believer, Agnes? She was attempting to do the work of the Holy Spirit without the power of the Holy Spirit. Although God was blessing her faith with healing power and increasing ministry, she was being drained of her strength trying to carry out this work.

Through the leading of the Lord, Agnes and some friends gathered to ask God for the fullness of His Spirit. They laid hands on each other and prayed for the coming of the Holy Spirit. Agnes said, "The power of the Spirit fell upon us immediately."[29]

One of the first signs of the Spirit's fullness was the presence of supernatural strength. Agnes noticed that the Spirit brought "within the very flesh the capacity to receive the power of God." This was important because Agnes' ministry was about to move into a new level of effectiveness and recognition. The baptism of the Holy Spirit brought gifts and joy. But most important the fullness brought power. Thus everything in mind and body was "quickened, made more alert and more efficient."

The same conditions of emptying and filling must be met if we are to know this strength of Jesus. The Holy Spirit empties believers of a dependence upon their human strength. He does it by calling them into some activity that they are incapable of doing by human power. He calls them to witness to an individual or pray for the sick. The Holy Spirit prompts these believers into a situation where God's power must show up or they will fail. They are tempted to resist the Spirit's prompting because they don't want to take the risk and do what He is asking them to do. But that is the very reason He calls them to do it. He is emptying out all self-dependence. He is answering their prayer to be filled with the Holy Spirit.

It is not enough however, that they discover their inadequacy. Believers who are Spirit-filled must exercise faith in God's adequacy. They then need to ask Him for His gifts, that they might help those who desperately need the touch of His power. They receive an infusion of His power to do His ministry.

All this emptying of self-dependence and filling with His power isn't a one-time experience. It begins with an initial act of faith for His fullness and continues in a process of obedience as the Spirit leads.

A Full Heart

When the Holy Spirit comes in His fullness, He also fills the hearts of believers with a passion for God. This love for the Lord becomes so dominant that these believers even begin to choose against their own desires for this burning affection.

How does the Holy Spirit do this? First, He will empty their hearts of primary affections that need to be secondary. The Holy Spirit reveals love for self, personal indulgence, pleasure and security. They are asked to repent of their selfish participation in these passions. Total obedience and surrender empties the heart of these dominant loves.

The Spirit wants to empty their hearts so He may fill it with a deeper passion for their heavenly Father. Believers should not fear this full surrender. Paul says in Romans 8:15-16,

> *"For you did not receive a spirit that makes you a slave again to fear, but you receive the Spirit of sonship. And by him we cry, 'Abba', Father. The Spirit himself testifies with our spirit that we are God's children."*

The Holy Spirit gives these believers a greater capacity to enjoy the intimacy of divine presence. If they withdraw from this work because it seems too mystical or fanatical they will quench the work of the Holy Spirit in their lives. The Spirit longs to fill their hearts so they will love God supremely.

Jeanne, the incomplete believer, was struggling with the continued pull toward sin in her life. She came to a place where she made an absolute commitment to die to her selfish affections. This decision was followed by a series of difficult events that stripped her of pride and self-interest. Then God came in His cleansing power to change the affections of her life. "That heart, where I formally detected in the secret places so many evil motives, was now so far as I was enabled to perceive, made pure."

Jeanne emptied herself of old affections and God filled her with His affections. She explained, "The principle of action did not seem to be from motives applied without, but rather to be involved in a life springing up and operative within. All was done in God, and it was done quietly, freely, naturally, continually."[30]

Spirit-filled believers understand that God forgives in order to deliver. He has given the Holy Spirit in order to fill with the Holy Spirit. He wants to make every believer like His Son, and Spirit-filled believers seek what God wants.

As the Spirit guides they surrender each area of their lives to Him. Just as he asked Sam, Agnes and Jeanne, He asks them to surrender ground that is very important to their self-interests. After prayer and faith He gives them the power to choose His will over their own. He gives them the strength to vote with Him, against themselves.

Like these believers when we ask and trust the Holy Spirit to fill us, He can give us the mind of Jesus. By crossing frontiers that are beyond our strength, God's power will break through our lives. When we choose to sacrifice selfish pleasure, the Spirit of Holiness can draw us into the fullness of God's presence by the pull of His burning passion.

The Holy Spirit wants to manifest the character of Jesus in your heart. He wants the love of God to overflow the banks of your spirit through the fullness of the Holy Spirit. This is the great work of God that not only changes our lives, but the countless lives that surround us. To every one of us God says, "I want to make you like this. Let me complete My work in you. Be filled with the Holy Spirit."

PART 3

The Gallery of Churches

In the galleries of sinners and believers we saw some portraits of individuals. Now in this gallery we will see three more portraits. But these are not the portraits of individuals. These are group portraits of churches. A church is a community of believers. And here is the exciting truth: in a greater degree than a single individual, a church more fully manifests the transforming power of Jesus Christ.

Like sinners and believers churches also have different features. These features differ according to the level of the Spirit's power in our churches. One of the portraits in this gallery reveals a complete loss of spiritual power in a church. Another one portrays some strong signs of the Holy Spirit's presence, but also some hidden dangers in the thinking of the people.

Finally, there is a portrait of ongoing transformation. It is a group of believers seeking the Spirit's activity as well as His wisdom. These people understand what Paul proclaims in Romans 9:16, when he says,

> "It does not, therefore, depend on man's desire or effort, but on God's mercy."

This is the portrait of a church depending on God's mercy while living in both revival and maturity.

It would be good for us to examine these portraits regularly. Then we would see if our churches are experiencing all that Jesus wants to do in us as His body.

Chapter 9

Hardened Churches

"God gave them a spirit of stupor..."
(Romans 11:8)

"All the churches are passing through a period of unusual dullness."[31]
(H.K. Carroll)

❧ ☙

"Ignoring the Supernatural"

The first portrait in the gallery of churches displays very little life. The main feature of this portrait is hardness. How do a group of people who once knew the power and presence of God become hardened? That was the question A.M. Hills tried to answer.

A.M. Hills lived through a very powerful move of the Holy Spirit that changed the spiritual landscape of the country. It was a period marked by great faith and divine activity in countless churches. But now there was a hardening in many of these churches and A.M. Hills gave himself to alerting people about the hardening that was taking place.

He was not the only one to see it. A Christian magazine of His day reported, "We have one dire disease – spiritual famine – lack of the witness of the Spirit, lack of personal experience, lack of spiritual power."[32] The church was becoming sophisticated and rich. People were no longer seeking opportunities to believe Jesus Christ. These churches were now self-dependent. The leaders of one group of churches lamented that the power of God had passed away and self-interest and entertainment had softened these churches. "The heart searching that once prepared the way for the work of revival," they reported, "is often avoided as fanaticism."[33]

A.M. Hills tried to point out to these hardened churches that many of them were in decline and some barely growing. He was convinced that one of the primary reasons for this hardening was in the leadership. "The truth is," he said, "the theological professors and those who are responsible for the training of the ministry, and the men high up in ecclesiastical power in our denomination, are, almost without exception magnifying the natural and ignoring the supernatural. They are making a great deal of talent and education and oratory, and in equal measure they are discounting the importance of the baptism with the Holy Spirit."[34] Churches were slowly, almost imperceptibly fossilizing!

At one time hardened churches saw the manifest power of the Holy Spirit, but now they no longer see such divine activity. There was a day when they witnessed sinners becoming believers by the power of God. In those days they saw believers filled with the Holy Spirit in order to resist sin and manifest the character and ministry of Jesus Christ. But these fundamental works of the Spirit began to diminish and finally disappeared altogether. Now there is no sign of divine activity in these assemblies. There maybe a lot of human activity, but there is no divine activity. They are hardened to the work of God.

We need to understand what brings these communities of believers to such a condition. It doesn't matter whether churches have been like this for generations or a few months because the hardness can be reversed.

God Chooses to Harden

Hardened churches do not see God's activity because God Himself has chosen not to be active in their assemblies. Romans 9:18 tells us,

> "Therefore God has mercy on whom he wants to have mercy, and he hardens whom he wants to harden."

They are hardened because God chooses to harden them. Other congregations experience the favor of God because God chooses to bless them.

When God chooses to show His favor on a people, they soar in His power. It does not matter how poor they are. It matters little how ignorant or weak they are. When God chooses favor, then the Kingdom of God will erupt into their lives with supernatural force.

The opposite is also true. If God chooses hardness, the Spirit's activity is going to fade out of those assemblies. Churches can have financial resources, buildings and education, but if God chooses hardness, these things will not bring divine activity to them.

It is like a plane in flight. As long as there is power in the engines it will soar. The power is God's favor. The plane can be filled with ignorant, poor and uncultured people, but if the engines roar, these people will fly. Without the power the plane will crash, even if it is filled with educated, cultured and religious professionals. It is God's choice to release or withhold His power in a church.

The Condition of Hardness

Churches are hardened because God chooses to shut down His power. Does this mean there is nothing for hardened churches to do but buckle their seat belt and wait for the crash?

No! Although it is true that God chooses favor or hardness for a people, His choice is based on certain conditions. God chooses favor for those people who believe and He chooses hardness for the people who achieve. Faith is the condition for God's favor. Self-dependence is the condition for hardness.

Paul explains why the Gentiles are experiencing God's favor and Israel is experiencing hardness. He says in Romans 9:30–32,

> *"That the Gentiles, who did not pursue righteousness, have obtained it, a righteousness that is by faith; but Israel, who pursued a law of righteousness, has not attained it. Why not? Because they pursued it not by faith but as if it were by works."*

Faith in God brings mercy whereas human activity brings hardness.

Hardened churches are very active in religious work. Many of their members have committed their time, energy and resources for God. All of their lives are marked by high, energy output in a religious environment. But they do not believe the Lord for anything! And therein lies the problem.

They strive after high and worthy goals. These churches want to be good and do good things for God. They are very active in seeking to reach these high goals, but it is all done by human effort. It does not matter how active these churches are, or how high their goals are; God will not endorse their self-dependence with His power and presence. God hardens churches when they refuse to believe His Son for anything. It's true they are religious people in big religious buildings doing a lot of religious activity. But there is no faith.

Changing the Conditions

Please understand. God has not rejected these people, He has only hardened them. There is a big difference. In Romans 11:1–2 Paul discusses the hardening of Israel and asks,

> "Did God reject his people? By no means! God did not reject his people who he foreknew."

As with Israel God simply refuses to manifest His Spirit's activity among hardened churches because they no longer believe. It is not rejection. He has cut down the power to get their attention. It is His attempt to wake them up to the fact that they don't believe Him like they once did.

This absence of the Holy Spirit's activity would only be for a season if these churches would repent of self-dependence and begin to believe Jesus Christ again. The standard of success as the people of God is not found in religious buildings, activities or record-breaking attendance. Success is measured by the demonstration of God's activity and nature in the life of the assembly. This only comes by faith.

These hardened churches need to get around people of faith. When they relate to people who believe the Lord for His

Spirit's work, it makes hardened churches envious for what God is doing in believing churches. Then they begin to believe the Lord for these manifestations in their own community.

Throughout history God has used an individual of faith or a people of faith to bring hardened churches to belief again. If hardened churches have no such people around them, they should seek believing people so they will be encouraged toward faith.

There is a bottom-line question for every group of believers. Is God's Spirit active today like your church once knew Him to be? If not, God is choosing to harden your church. He has not rejected it; rather He is only pulling back His Spirit to get your attention. It is time for your church to exercise faith in Jesus Christ and call upon the Lord once again for the manifestation of His mighty power and presence.

Chapter 10

Wild Churches

*"You, though a wild olive shoot,
have been grafted in among the others..."*
(Romans 11:17)

*"Their numbers increase,
and their wild pranks are beyond description."*[35]
(David Lloyd)

~~~~~

"They Are Stark Mad"

In the first portrait of this gallery we saw churches that are hardened. Now in the second portrait we'll see "wild churches". The folks in this portrait believe God and have a zeal for Him, but sometimes their zeal goes to an extreme. When churches enter a season of extreme zeal things get wild. Such a revival movement was reported in several parts of Wales. This work was characterized by extended periods of praise and worship throughout many churches.

In the excitement of this revival a phenomena appeared that seemed somewhat wild to the world and even to other churches. The people in their joy would jump before the Lord. Criticism began to increase because of such behavior. "It appears to all true and serious Christians," said one critic, "that they are stark mad, and given to a spirit of delusion, to the great disgrace and scandal of Christianity."[36]

In spite of the criticism and misunderstanding the revival

brought many to Jesus Christ and hundreds into the ministry. The untidiness of the work was simply the new believers giving "vent to the spiritual energy which was in their breasts."[37] This energy changed lives, homes and communities.

Maybe the best response to the criticism leveled at those wild churches was given by one of the preachers: "You English blame us, the Welsh, and speak against us and say 'Jumpers! Jumpers!' but we, the Welsh, have something also to allege against you, and we must justly say of you, 'Sleepers! Sleepers!' "[38] It is far better to have a church full of jumping believers than sleeping members!

Though churches may not be filled with jumping members, they can still be wild churches made up of new believers who enthusiastically come together. Because many of the people are fresh in their experience of becoming believers or being filled with the Spirit, they are full of faith. They believe God to work mightily in their midst, and He does. Many of these wild churches have no tradition of truth. Nevertheless, they believe the Lord for His divine activity and He favors them with His power and presence.

Wild churches need to understand that their wildness is due to an explosive faith and enthusiasm over the divine power in their lives. This is good. But wildness can also come from a faith that is out of control. Without discipline and discernment, spiritual energy can drive them into countless problems and difficulties. Here are some common attitudes churches should avoid, for the health of their assembly.

Stay Humble

They should not become arrogant. As wild churches look around and see the great manifestation of the Spirit's power in their congregation they are tempted to boast. It will be easy for them to conclude that they are better people than those in hardened churches. But the Holy Spirit is not active in these wild churches because they are better than others. Nor does His activity make them superior to hardened churches. The divine activity they witness is a gift from God to people who believe. They are not superior, rather they believe and the hardened churches do not.

In Romans 11:19-20 Paul speaks of this arrogant boasting. He says,

> *"You will say then, 'Branches were broken off so that I could be grafted in.' Granted. But they were broken off because of unbelief, and you stand by faith."*

God's blessing on wild churches is not an invitation for them to boast over those churches He is not favoring. Such boasting will turn to criticism of hardened churches. Then they will write them off as a lost cause, becoming hardened toward the hardened. Such an attitude is of no benefit to hardened people or to the fulfillment of God's purpose.

Please understand that wild churches are the only hope for hardened churches to get back to faith. Instead of ignoring them, wild churches should make these other churches jealous for what God is doing. As they open their lives to hardened people and the hardened churches witness the Spirit's power, those hardened churches can become curious about the work of God. As hardened people see God's work in wild churches, they may become hungry for this divine activity and begin to explore how they can experience His power. If wild churches however, refuse to associate with these people, hardened churches may never turn to faith.

Again wild churches must not become arrogant. They should continue to believe God for His mighty works in their midst and share their life with others who do not believe. Arrogance can derail wild churches from faith and keep others from believing. It is important that wild churches stay humble and open.

Live Scared

These churches should also avoid being over confident. Paul sternly warns in Romans 11:20-21,

> *"Do not be arrogant, but be afraid. For if God did not spare the natural branches, he will not spare you either."*

When the Spirit's activity is being manifested it becomes easy to presume that God will always manifest His power and presence in wild churches. They need to live with a healthy fear. They should remember that even hardened churches lived in the power of the Spirit at one time. Hardened churches were once wild churches, but they gradually lost their faith. Soon the activity of the Spirit ceased. It happens quickly and it can happen to all churches!

It doesn't hurt to live scared. This doesn't mean wild churches have to be paranoid about losing their faith. But they should have a healthy fear and respect of those things that can rob them of their faith in Jesus Christ.

The enemy can lead them away from faith by deceit. Since he can't keep wild churches from believing the Lord he will try to get them to believe for experiences that are not of the Lord. Wild churches are particularly vulnerable at this point. Satan can tempt them into presumption, where they believe beyond the Word of God. Faith alone is not their security, rather faith in what the Lord Jesus is calling them to believe. Wild churches need to measure every experience by the Word of God.

The world can tempt them to exchange their faith for material things and securities. Soon they are no longer choosing opportunities in which to believe God, but they are seeking havens of comfort. If they do not fight it, the gravitational pull of the world will draw wild churches away from faith toward well-being and security.

Selfish desires can also rob them of faith. There will be times when they are tempted to easily solve problems by themselves and with expediency instead of believing God in the face of difficulty. Then problems will no longer be solved by the power of the Spirit, but by human expertise and resources. They will quickly become an assembly that is self-dependent, rather than a people believing the Lord for His difficult and sacrificial will. Expediency can eat away at faith.

Wild churches are exciting congregations. But lack of knowledge, discipline and discernment can lead to disaster. Others were once wild churches but are now hardened. Wild churches should avoid arrogance and boasting at all costs. They shouldn't become over-confident in the signs of God's favor. They too can be hardened if they forget to believe the Lord Jesus Christ for His mighty works.

Paul says in Romans 11:22,

> *"Consider therefore the kindness and sternness of God: sternness to those who fell, but kindness to you, provided that you continue in his kindness."*

If you are part of a wild church, the only security for your church is to believe what Jesus Christ is calling all of you to do. It will go cross grain with the enemy's temptations, the world's allurements, and everyone's selfish desires, but your church must trust the Lord. Wild churches should believe and live scared!

Chapter 11

Renewed Churches

"So too, at the present time there is a remnant chosen by grace."
(Romans 11:5)

"In their faces there shone the radiance of divine grace, so that by their means a great work was achieved."[39]
(Cinozzi)

"Fire within Me"

The dominant feature of this portrait is ever-increasing transformation. Here is the portrait of renewed churches. Throughout history this kind of church has brought life to countless people and communities. Renewed churches have broken free from the bondage of hardness.

It had been a long time since the hardened church of Florence heard the voice of the Lord. This church was seeking to survive in a society of outward refinement and moral decay. Unfortunately, the disintegration of the moral fiber of the culture was invading the church. One of Florence's leading citizens exclaimed, "We have become void of religion and corrupt."[40]

Into this hardened setting the voice of Jesus Christ came through Girolamo, a young friar who filled the pulpit of St. Mark's in Florence. As the Lord began to speak to him, he at first was hesitant to report what the Spirit was saying. "I sought," he wrote, "no longer to speak in thy name, O Lord, but Thou has overpowered me, has conquered me. Thy word has become like a fire within me, consuming the very marrow of my bones."[41]

He preached the prophetic word with boldness and people began to respond. An observer wrote, "On the days when the friar of St. Mark preached, the streets were almost a desert; houses, schools and shops were closed."[42] Grace was coming to Florence and many were converted. A remnant of God's people was being raised up in a world of darkness and sin.

Renewed churches are beginning to believe again. They are thawing out from a season of hardness and seeking to regain faith. These congregations are on the stretch to once more see the Spirit's manifest presence and power.

Renewed churches have the best of both worlds. They are opening up to the new thing God is doing with all the energy that comes in a contemporary move of the Holy Spirit. But they are also bringing to that experience a rich tradition and history of truth that will help them navigate with precision.

It is no wonder that throughout church history these communities have guided the great movements of revival. Renewed churches blend together openness to the fresh eruptions of the Spirit and have the ability not to be detoured from God's ways and truth.

If divine life is to return to hardened congregations, these churches must return to the primitive faith. Intensity of religious activity, abundance of resources, and increase in attendance are not the measure for the progress of churches. Rather renewed churches seek what originally transformed them into the people of God.

Ears to Hear

In the beginning they listened to the Lord's voice. In Romans 10:17 Paul makes it clear where renewing faith comes from. He says,

> *"Consequently, faith comes from hearing the message, and the message is heard through the word of Christ."*

What the Spirit is saying is absolutely essential. Without His voice churches will no longer have the Lord Jesus' direction.

And without His guidance they will turn to religious activity to fill their time and justify their existence. As they heard Jesus Christ's voice when they first believed so all churches must continue to hear His voice. They must be committed to hearing the Lord through both biblical truth and the prophetic ministry of the Holy Spirit. They should seek to listen!

At the height of Girolamo's ministry, he gave a challenge: "Florence! Jesus Christ, who is King of the universe, hath willed to become thy King. Wilt thou have Him for thy King?" The people sensed they had heard the voice of the Lord and responded in faith, "Jesus Christ our King!" The voice of God had brought them life.

Hearts to Believe

Next, renewed churches believe what Jesus Christ has revealed to them through His voice. Romans 10:14 asks,

> "How, then, can they call on the one they have not believed in? And how can they believe in the one of whom they have not heard?"

Once they hear, then renewed churches believe the Lord for what He says. They don't just believe for an initial experience but for a continuous work. Their faith expresses itself through prayer. The prayer life of renewed churches is ever increasing and central to all that happens.

Also, they confess what they believe through words and actions. What these churches speak and do erupts out of believing hearts. There is expectation in their assemblies that God is going to show up and do His will in the congregation. Such expectation spreads through their churches by confession.

Like cold, hard tundra that is coming back to life under the spring sun, renewed churches begin to see the supernatural signs of the Spirit's presence under their shining faith. People are coming to faith in Jesus Christ; believers are being filled with the Holy Spirit. Prayer and praise begin to dominate the environment and these churches capture a vision of what Jesus Christ wants to do.

Eyes to See

Now here are some signs churches need to watch for so that you don't abort the work of renewal. They must avoid the Elijah complex. In Romans 11:3 Paul quotes Elijah when he says,

> "I am the only one left and they are trying to kill me."

Elijah was a prophet who became overwhelmed with the odds. He thought he was the only prophet left. He became very depressed. Churches too can get depressed and even bitter when they are always focusing on how few believe. Renewed churches are smaller groups in a landscape filled with hardened churches. But they shouldn't end up sulking about how few they are. They need to focus on Jesus Christ, not the odds. The Lord has always used small groups to change the course of His Church. Renewed churches are generally in the footnotes of church history but they are the true catalyst for the work of God in its day. These churches must believe and stay focused on the Lord Jesus Christ.

Renewed churches exercise their faith in what the Lord can do for them. Jesus Christ will manifest His activity more and more as they believe more and more. They create opportunities to believe the Spirit for His work in their congregation. These churches place themselves in situations where they have to depend on God. As they grow in faith, they also grow in the work of the Spirit. Renewed churches will increase the opportunities and occasions to believe God.

Finally, they don't become hardened toward hardened churches. If hardened churches ever get back into faith they can become an incredible army of believers. Paul reminds us in Romans 11:23 that there is hope for the hardened. He says,

> "If they do not persist in unbelief, they will be grafted in, for God is able to graft them in again."

Renewed churches don't criticize these people. Rather, they make them jealous for the work that the Spirit is doing. They invite and encourage hardened churches back into faith. They can be the bridge for hardened people to come into renewal.

Renewed churches avoid bitterness, grow in faith and go after the hardened. They will be able to keep on course and God will be able to use them powerfully if they follow these simple guidelines.

The church must be continually renewed, so this portrait is for every church. If your church senses loss of faith in its life and the diminishing of the mighty works of God, it is receiving the first signals of hardness. Pull together with some believers. Begin to listen to the Lord and believe Him for what He wants to do. All of you give yourselves to faith and obedience and God will begin to renew your congregation. This is the work He delights to do for His church.

PART 4

The Gallery of Disciples

In this final gallery of portraits each portrait has a feature that reflects the very nature of Jesus Christ. They are all portraits of disciples. Disciples believe Jesus Christ for the forgiveness of their sins and for His divine life. They are also receiving the fullness of the Holy Spirit. And they link themselves with other Spirit-filled believers in a community of faith.

Disciples are passionate followers of the Lord Jesus Christ. This love is creating an environment for the character of Jesus Christ to blossom in them.

How does this happen? Because of their passion for Jesus Christ they are sacrificing what others protect. In this rich mixture of sacrifice and worship, God does an awesome miracle. Paul says in Romans 12:1,

> *"Therefore, I urge you brothers, in view of God's mercy offer your bodies as living sacrifices, holy and pleasing to God – this is your spiritual act of worship."*

Look at each portrait and see how the fruits of Jesus' character are developing out of their sacrifice of worship. All of these are portraits of transformation.

Chapter 12

Humble Disciples

"Do not be conceited."
(Romans 12:16)

"I have not the insufferable conceit to suppose that it was anything in me that drew them."[43]
(Catherine Booth-Clibborn)

∽ ∾

"You Have Killed Ridicule"

This portrait is very rare yet it has the one feature that God desires in all His children. The dominant feature of this portrait is humility. In the disciples who have this characteristic there is a striking resemblance to Jesus' character. Catherine Booth-Clibbon had the Christ-like feature of humility.

In Catherine's passion to bring a lost world to Jesus Christ she had ministered among the discarded people in society. At times she had been ridiculed, mocked and even put in jail, but God had blessed her faithfulness with the salvation of many of those people.

Once while she was ministering, the Lord gave her the direction to "go to Brussels; go in sackcloth and ashes; go and tell of sin; let everything in your person speak of sin and awaken conscience; then proclaim, behold the Lamb of God, that taketh away the sins of the world."[44] When Catherine shared with her colleagues that she was to go to Brussels and appear in sackcloth, they were shocked and told her she must not do it. She responded, "I am going to live these three weeks as if they were my last on earth. I have left my home and little ones and am going to exist for this town. If Christ laid down His life for us, we have got to lay down our lives for the salvation of Brussels."[45]

Pride is an addiction to selfish interest. It is the dominant goal and driving force behind much human activity. But sacrificed pride is the unique mark of passionate lovers of Jesus Christ. Humility defines disciples who are learning to live without an addiction to selfishness.

This rare expression of Jesus' character is produced in humble disciples. It only grows if, like Catherine, they give up self-interest. The behavior portrayed here is not the kind the world produces, or even likes, but it is the behavior that the Holy Spirit creates. Humble disciples give the Spirit room to produce Jesus' likeness. It happens when they sacrifice the following areas of self-interest.

Take Down the Ladder

They give up any attempt to boost their personal recognition in the church. In Romans 12:3 Paul warns,

"I say to every one of you: Do not think of yourself more highly than you ought, rather think of yourself with sober judgment, in accordance with the measure of faith God has given you."

Paul gives this warning because pride causes some believers to transform the church into a ladder for spiritual fame. It propels them to climb higher and higher over fellow believers. They have no satisfaction until they are on top, recognized above everyone else. These folks not only seek to elevate personal recognition; they also work to maintain the top position.

Humble disciples refuse to elevate themselves. The church is not a ladder for spiritual fame; rather it is the body of Christ. God has given them a function, a measure of faith and a place to do their unique ministry. Fulfillment is not found in jockeying for a bigger and better position. Joy for disciples only comes from doing what God calls them to do and doing it with their whole heart.

They understand that if God has placed them in a prominent position, it is not for self-recognition but for the sake of His body. On the other hand, humble disciples are aware that if God has placed them in an obscure ministry, it has nothing to do with their worth but everything to do with His plan.

There will always be some believers who plan and plot their place in the church to bring to them greater recognition. But it doesn't matter how much they are doing for God, their life is still a tribute to themselves instead of a living and holy sacrifice, pleasing to God. Remember God delights in the aroma of sacrificed pride.

Sacrificed Reputation

Humble disciples give up protecting their reputations. Pride causes us to be concerned about how critics perceive us. Soon, we act or don't act because of the way it will be received by friends and critics. This unhealthy concern for reputation causes us to live by the dictates of peer pressure.

Remember Catherine's call to sacrifice her reputation? The night of the first meeting in Brussels she put on a coarse robe with a single seam and smeared real ashes on her face. As she waited to go out the enemy tempted her. She began to think that she could not have done anything more stupid than what she was about to do. She wondered what people would think and how foolish she was to assume the role of a prophet. Catherine became paralyzed with fear wondering if she had made a mistake.

But a friend told her to go on because she was doing what God instructed her to do. When she walked on the stage the audience was stunned in silence. She spoke from the depth of her spirit and this began a two-month campaign that moved the entire city toward Jesus Christ. A prominent citizen said to Catherine, "Everybody has been ridiculed here except you. Ridicule kills everything; you have killed ridicule."[46]

Like Catherine, humble disciples give up protecting their reputations. Romans 12:16 says,

> "Do not be proud, but be willing to associate with people of low position. Do not be conceited."

Humble disciples do what they do, not because of how people will accept them, but because love for Jesus demands it. They are determined to hate what is evil and embrace the good, even if everyone else says they are being old fashioned. These humble disciples seek greater spiritual fervor and zeal when those around accuse them of being fanatics. They associate with people who are broken and poor even though others may hint that they are losers for doing it. And they refuse to promote themselves while the world calls them failures.

There are believers who expend great amounts of energy positioning themselves so that others will accept them. They are more concerned with what people think than what Jesus wants. To avoid such a life, humble disciples sacrifice their reputations! The world will never be happy with anyone who is absolutely committed to Jesus Christ. These believers have decided that the pleasure of God will motivate their actions instead of the world's acceptance.

Don't Even the Score

Finally, humble disciples give up revenge. Pride answers any damage to our self-interest with a return volley. It matters little whether the ammunition is criticism, angry words or harsh actions. Evil, many of us believe, must be met with swift and immediate reprisal. Otherwise such unanswered action could destroy our self-esteem.

But humble disciples refuse to repay those who hurt them with more hurt. As a matter of fact, they don't just commit to silence, but they respond with good to those who do them wrong. The defense mechanism of anger is dismantled and replaced with a constant flow of peace even to those who are hurtful.

There are other believers who seek to even the score against those who have done wrong to them. Humble disciples however, observe the hardest dimension of sacrificed pride and the posture most like Jesus. They worship by the offering of their self-interest and it brings great joy to the heart of God. Paul speaks the truth in Romans 12:19 when he says,

> *"Do not take revenge, my friends, but leave room for God's wrath, for it is written, 'It is mine to avenge; I will repay,' says the Lord."*

Here is the portrait of humble disciples. If you want this portrait, sacrifice any attempt to boost your recognition, protect your reputation and seek revenge. Make pride an offering totally consumed by your burning passion for Jesus Christ. Your offering will greatly please the Lord!

Chapter 13

Submissive Disciples

"Everyone must submit himself to the governing authorities for there is no authority except that which God has established."
(Romans 13:1)

"It became clear to us through the Scriptures that our resistance was to be that of overcoming evil with good."[47]
(Festo Kivengere)

~~~

"Losing My Liberty"

Submissive disciples are hard to encounter today. The feature of this portrait looks amazingly similar to the submission in our Lord Jesus Christ. Here is a likeness worthy of our wholehearted pursuit. Festo Kivengere sought this feature with a fiery zeal.

Festo lived under a dictator who had recently come to power and was determined to make the country Muslim. A violent persecution broke out against all Christians that made up about 80 percent of the nation. As churches searched the Scriptures and heard the Lord they determined not to violently resist the persecution although they were willing to quietly resist in some areas. "This included refusing to cooperate with anything that dehumanizes," wrote Festo, "but we reaffirmed that we can never be involved in using force."[48]

In the white heat of persecution the leader of Festo's church was executed. Festo was the next leader on the government hit list. His people encouraged him to escape the country. Miraculously, he and his family made it out.

While outside his country, grieving with pain over the death of his friends, he noticed hatred toward the president of his home country was strangling his spiritual life. "I grew increasingly bitter," he confessed, "and was, to the same degree, losing my liberty and my ministry."[49]

The Lord spoke a strong word to Festo to forgive the dictator even as the Lord Jesus forgave those who executed Him. After a long struggle Festo forgave. Because of the Lord's immeasurable grace, Festo testified, he loved the president of the country, forgave him and was praying for him.

Like Festo, submissive disciples sacrifice their personal rights as an expression of their worship to the living God. The world says they don't have to give up these rights. Even some believers question whether such rights ought to be sacrificed in every situation. But if these disciples are going to submit to God's ways then certain rights must be forever dismissed. In their desire to please God there is no other option but sacrifice.

Because Jesus calls His disciples to trust His authority, the altar of their lives will hold the charred remains of three sacrificed rights. Here are the rights that submissive disciples sacrifice.

The Right to Rebel

They sacrifice the right to rebel against a governing authority. Now, other believers may agree that submission to a governing authority is good. However, if that authority begins to act in ways contrary to the will of God, then they argue that people should use their right to rebel, in order to dismantle the threatening structure.

But submissive disciples believe the governing authority over them exists because God has instituted it for social order. To destroy an existing authority is to presume the power of God. Only God dismisses governments and brings them into existence. Therefore these disciples have no right to rebel against their governing authority. In Romans 13:1–2 Paul explains,

"The authorities that exist have been established by God. Consequently, he who rebels against the authority is rebelling against what God has instituted, and those who do so will bring judgment on themselves."

Submissive disciples can protest against the activities of a governing authority. They can escape from its borders. These believers can even disobey laws that are contrary to God's laws, if they are willing to submit to the authorities' punishments. They can also seek to change its laws through governmental procedure. But they never choose to dismantle the authority over them through the power of rebellion.

During those great persecutions that Festo experienced, the churches were never closed down. As a matter of fact, they were constantly crowded with believers. Yet had they been closed, the churches would have continued. Festo explained, "... the life of the Body of Christ would have gone right on in the love-fellowship, meetings in secret and in the predawn home worship that kept our eyes focused on the Lord Jesus and our hearts bowed before His cross."[50]

For some, the sacrifice of the right to rebel will mean very little. For others it will cost them their freedom or even their lives. Not all believers have moved into this high altitude of obedience. But for those who have, it is a testimony to the greatest power of all: the power to suffer and die for the glory of God.

The Right to Harm

Like Festo, submissive disciples do away with their rights to intentionally harm another person. Paul is crystal clear in Romans 13:10 when he says,

"Love does no harm to its neighbor."

With objection, other folks explain that they will have to harm some people to survive in this world. It can't be helped. Even believers give in to subtle forms of harming others by criticism or gossip. It seems inevitable.

Nevertheless, submissive disciples take the right to harm

out of their lives. God is calling them to live under the authority of love. This means that harming someone is no longer an option.

No doubt there will be times when they hurt other people. Through a mistake, conviction or tough decision others will be hurt. But they never *seek* to harm others. They do not destroy relationships, break commitments, shatter trusts, take a life, or damage minds. They choose to love their neighbors as themselves. To harm another person is now just as unthinkable as harming their own lives.

The exchange of our power to harm for His power to love is one of the great transactions of a sacrificial life. Because submissive disciples choose to live under the authority of love, they refuse to exercise the right to harm.

The Right to Sin

Finally, submissive disciples sacrifice the right to intentionally sin against God. Some believers claim this is impossible. They insist that we inevitably are going to sin every day in thought, word and deed, because there is no way to consistently resist the desires of our sinful nature. But, there is a way. It is found in the power of the Holy Spirit and our commitment to access by faith the holy life of Jesus Christ who dwells within us by the presence of His Spirit. In their choice to submit to the covering of a holy life, submissive disciples sacrifice their right to gratify any sinful desires.

In Romans13: 12–14 there is a call to give up the right to sin. Paul says,

> *"So let us put aside the deeds of darkness and put on the armor of light. Let us behave decently, as in the daytime, not in orgies and drunkenness, not in sexual immorality and debauchery, not in dissension and jealousy. Rather, clothe yourselves with the Lord Jesus Christ, and do not think about how to gratify the desires of the sinful nature."*

Now, there will be times when we sin unintentionally and there may be times when we stumble and react out of our old habits and patterns. The Lord can and will forgive us as we come to him in repentance. But submissive disciples daily seek a life that is committed by the power of the Spirit to lay aside the deeds of darkness and to put on the covering of light. In order to do that, there is an intentional decision to sacrifice their right to sin.

The world puts a high premium on the accumulation of rights. A life of sacrificed rights stand out in stark contrast. As a submissive disciple make your obedience to God's order, love and holiness more important to you than retaining your personal rights. Offer up to God through the work of the Spirit a holy sacrifice of your right to rebel, to harm and to sin. Your offering will greatly please God.

Chapter 14

Tender Disciples

"Let us therefore make every effort to do what leads to peace and to mutual edification."
(Romans 14:19)

"When it came to spiritual matters I thought I had the only way. But my way wasn't necessarily God's way."[51]
(Bruce Olson)

⨯⨯⨯

"Hating the Song"

Tender disciples have a characteristic desperately needed today. In a world that pursues personal agendas this portrait is a refreshing breeze from the kingdom of God. Bruce Olson was struggling to develop this feature in his life.

Bruce was a missionary seeking to bring a tribe of South American Indians, the *Montilone*, to faith in Jesus Christ. He had frequently risked his life to make contact with these people. Now, after living with them and learning their language and beautiful culture, he was praying for a conversion. The breakthrough came in a young man he called Bobby.

But Bobby would not share with the rest of the tribe his newfound faith in Jesus Christ. Bruce tried to encourage Bobby to speak to his people but he refused. "I wanted him to do things the way they would have been done in North America. I wanted him to call a meeting and tell about Jesus or corner his friends and explain what Jesus now meant to him."[52] Bobby continued to refuse and Bruce grew in his frustration.

The day did come, however, when Bobby shared his faith in a tribal festival. He did it through a wailing song that lasted fourteen hours. Bruce struggled with what he was doing. "I found myself hating the song." He said, "It sounded so heathen. The music, chanted in a strange minor key, sounded like witch music. It seemed to degrade the gospel."[53]

Like Bruce all of us have a personal preference for style of worship, structure of church, custom of faith and emphasis of doctrine. Although preferences change with individuals and churches, these things are not the indisputable truths of Scripture upon which we establish our faith and life. At times personal preferences can be points of conflict among individuals or churches. However, tender disciples will not use their preferences to harshly affect other people. Instead, they try to be gentle toward folks whose preferences are different than theirs.

It is not necessary for tender disciples to sacrifice their preferences when those preferences are in conflict with others, but they refuse to make them walls of alienation against others and the work of God. To avoid such alienation, they seek the following sacrifices.

Put Away the Measuring Stick

Tender disciples sacrifice any use of their preferences as a measure for God's work in the lives of other. Romans 14:1 says,

> "Accept him whose faith is weak, without passing judgment on disputable matters."

Only the Word of God is our measure. Yet there are some believers who use their lifestyle as a measuring stick for all other believers. These folks assume that if they are right, everyone else must be wrong. If they are spiritually mature everyone else must be immature. They use their preferences as the measure for truth instead of the Word of God.

But God works through a variety of ways in our lives. And there are many seasons of spiritual growth and change. So our position and experience as believers in the faith are not to be a means of judging. Tender disciples don't use their preferences to make others feel inferior or wrong. They give themselves to God in the way He is teaching them, but refuse to make their experiences the rule.

To cause others to feel wrong because of how Jesus works in our life would be to set our life as the measuring rod for everyone else's experience. Individual experiences, likes, customs, and perceptions make for a variety of ways in which God works through our lives. Therefore, tender disciples sacrifice any use of their preferences as a measure for other believers.

Put Away the Stumbling Block

They do not allow their preferences to be a stumbling block to others. Paul warns us in Romans 14:13,

> *"Therefore let us stop passing judgment on one another. Instead, make up your mind not to put any stumbling block or obstacle in your brother's way."*

Paul speaks this warning because some folks are going to do what they prefer even if it causes others to stumble and fall away from Jesus Christ. This doesn't mean their preferences are evil. They may simply show a measure of freedom or spiritual experience that a weaker person cannot handle. Yet, some believers still insist it is their right to live the way they choose no matter how it affects other folks.

Other believers are very tender to the weaknesses, misunderstandings and fears of the people around them. And if there is anything in their lifestyle that could cause problems for weaker believers, they sacrifice it for the sake of the weaker ones. Tender disciples do not seek some super-spiritual lifestyle that they have a right to live in all circumstances and situations. Rather, they seek a life in which they are always ministering righteousness, peace and joy in the Holy Spirit to those around them. While some claim the right to live out their preferences no matter how it affects others, these tender disciples seek to minister the Kingdom of God above their preferences. At times God will call them to make adjustments and sacrifices for the sake of those who do not understand. They choose to be sensitive in the company of others so weaker believers will not be confused or tempted.

Put Up No Limits

Finally, these disciples sacrifice any notion that their preferences are the limit of God's work. Some people are convinced they know all God has for them and that any lifestyle that goes beyond their experience is not of God. Their preferences are the end of the road for every believer.

Tender disciples refuse to set up their lives as the limit of God's work. They always are pressing into new frontiers and continually look to God's Word to see what He can teach them. They do not shut down a work of God even though it seems foreign from anything they have ever experienced. Romans 14:16 says, *"Do not allow what you consider good to be spoken of as evil."* That can happen when we use our good experiences as the limit of what God can do in other people's lives. It's important for tender disciples to trust God's greatness more than the comfort of their past experiences.

Bruce struggled over the strange way Bobby shared his faith in Jesus. Even though the people were captivated by the message of Jesus, Bruce wanted Bobby to stop. But God told Bruce to surrender his preferences and receive what the Spirit was doing. That night a wonderful revival of God's love was poured out on this tribe of Montilone Indians.

Because Bruce was tender toward God's rebuke and allowed Bobby to share through his tribal preferences many became believers in Jesus Christ. "God had spoken," remembers Bruce. "He had spoken in the Montilone language and through the Montilone culture."

Tender disciples are willing with Bruce to expose their lives to things that are uncomfortable, unpredictable and untidy. They refuse to allow their past and present preferences to be the limit of what God can do for them and others. Their personal preferences are not the end of God's work; therefore, they gladly sacrifice preferences for the new work of God in their lives!

We cannot survive without our personal preferences. They are the culture out of which we live. But as tender disciples we will never make these preferences the standard, the stumbling stone or the limit of the work of God to other people. A tenderness to minister the Kingdom of God should always take precedence over our personal preferences.

Chapter 15

Serving Disciples

"We who are strong ought to bear with the failings of the weak and not to please ourselves."
(Romans 15:1)

"Be a mother to them, and more than a mother. Watch over them tenderly, be just and kind."[54]
(from the cover of Amy Carmichael's Bible)

"Kneel Down Beside Him"

This portrait reflects one of the greatest features of Jesus Christ. It is the portrait of serving disciples. Amy Carmichael was discovering just how much this feature could overtake her life.

Amy had sacrificed the familiar surroundings of her home country and the riches of a developed nation to minister in another country. But now the Lord was calling her to sacrifice peace.

She was led by God to rescue little girls from the clutches of a perverted religious system that was sexually abusing and emotionally destroying their fragile lives. To obey meant she would attract the wrath of hell, the attack of these religious priests who were being robbed of their pleasure and the indictment of a society that accepted this practice as legal. To her surprise she was even shunned by fellow missionaries who felt she was upsetting a delicate environment for their ministry.

In the midst of her battle a vision came to Amy. She saw Jesus kneeling beneath an olive tree beside the place where she was keeping the children. He was praying for these children. She sensed the Lord was saying that the burden was not hers, but His. He was asking her to come and share His burden. "Who could have done anything," she wrote, "but go into the garden and kneel down beside Him under the olive tree?"[55]

Self-gratification is not always sin. But for Amy the ultimate goal in her life was to please God not herself. If it comes to a choice between grasping a pleasure or accepting God's call to minister, serving disciples will choose as Amy did to sacrifice their pleasures in order to engage in the ministry of God.

Look at those pleasures that can become a sacrifice of praise to God. Only a passion for Jesus and compassion for the world makes it possible for us to offer up these pleasures in worship.

Let the Familiar Go

The familiar is one of the great pleasures of life. It is hard for many believers to give themselves to different people, places and cultures. But believers should be ready to sacrifice the pleasure of the familiar as God directs them. Yes, there are some believers who fear change and cling to a predictable life. They refuse to go beyond the boundaries of the familiar. These folks will minister for the Lord, but only if they can do it in the comfort of familiar people and known surroundings.

Serving disciples also enjoy the surroundings of predictable people and familiar customs, but they determine to be torn loose from these in order to be obedient to God's call. They refuse to allow the familiar to limit the work of God through their lives. They live with the difficulty of unpredictable circumstances and unfamiliar people for the joy of seeing these very people encouraged in the faith of Jesus Christ. Paul, a Jew, reminds us of his call to go to unfamiliar people in Romans 15:16. He says God sent him,

> *"To be a minister of Christ Jesus to the Gentiles with the priestly duty of proclaiming the gospel of God, so that the*

Gentiles might become an offering acceptable to God, sanctified by the Holy Spirit."

Serving disciples listen for the call of God to minister. They seek to hear without any predetermined limits as to where they will minister. For them the pleasure of the predictable and familiar never blocks the pleasure of God. The Holy Spirit who ministers in the unfamiliar surroundings of a sinful world gives them the strength to sacrifice for the sake of that same world.

Let the Abundance Go

Indulgence is another gratification we protect. After all, we worked for it, earned it or inherited these resources, so why not enjoy them. A little indulgence in the good things of life is not all that bad. However, sacrificing disciples learn to sacrifice the pleasure of self-indulgence for the sake of helping those who have needs more important than their pleasures. When God directs them in terms of the sacrifice of this pleasure, they obey Him. Paul speaks of churches that knew how to sacrifice for the needs of others. In Romans 15:26–27 he reports,

> *"For Macedonia and Achaia were pleased to make a contribution for the poor among the saints in Jerusalem. They were pleased to do it, and indeed they owe it to them. For if the Gentiles have shared in the Jews' spiritual blessing, they owe it to the Jews to share with them their material blessings."*

In a world of abundance where indulgence is a way of life it becomes harder instead of easier to make this sacrifice. That is why sacrificing disciples seek the mind of the Lord concerning the resources that have come to their lives. They are convinced it should not be their selfish desires or even the surrounding needs of others that determine what they do with their resources. They listen for the voice of God. Needs get their attention but only God's voice gets their actions. When He moves upon their heart, they allow the sweet aroma of sacrificed indulgence to rise up toward heaven.

We serve a Savior who refused to indulge Himself in the pleasures of heaven. He sacrificed all so that He might lavish His wealth upon us. He is our model, but He is also our strength to do the same.

Let the Peace Go

No one is looking for a fight. And most of us will do all that is necessary to enjoy and maintain the pleasure of peace. But if God calls serving disciples into a battle for the sake of someone, then they lay down the pleasure of peace and enter into the conflict. At times these acts of ministry can disrupt their sleep, eating, comforts and friendships. But the issue at hand is not their comforts but the battle over the spiritual survival of an individual or group. Paul invites us into the battle for the sake of others. In Romans 15:30 he writes,

> *"I urge you, brothers, by our Lord Jesus Christ and by the love of the Spirit, to join me in my struggle by praying to God for me."*

The enemy of God will pound these disciples day and night if they choose to rob him of his work. It is a struggle. There is always peace and quiet far away from the front lines. But when the Lord calls, they sacrifice the peace and enter into the struggle.

Through the grueling battle that Amy entered, a day came when she was called to court to answer for her conduct of taking children from the temple. She defined that day as "the supreme hour of the long fight, the hour of utmost defeat, when for the first time we tasted public scorn, and knew how little we had drunk as yet the cup of our Savior's agony for souls."[56] She sacrificed the comfort of a safe ministry and went to the front line of conflict and suffering.

Like Amy, serving disciples leave their comforts, and join the conflict on the side of the God of peace. In the midst of the struggle He will minister a peace as He defeats the enemy. Romans 16:20 promises,

> *"The God of peace will soon crush Satan under your feet."*

In giving up a life without battles, serving disciples discover a greater peace that comes through a victorious battle against the enemy of God. The struggle is difficult but they gladly accept the orders of their Lord.

If we become these disciples who serve there will be a dramatic plate shift in our hearts. Our decisions will not be made for the pleasure of self but to encourage others and for the pleasure of God. This is God's work. As serving disciples we will give Him every opportunity to prove His work in our lives.

"The God of peace will be with you. Amen."
(Romans 15:33)

Conclusion

A Portrait Worth Praising

Photographs are an exact record of how people look. Portraits are not. Portraits don't record every detail. They simply interpret the appearance of people. Through a blend of light, colors, and features the artist brings out character qualities in order to interpret a subject.

But these portraits of spiritual transformation interpret something different than our character qualities. Each portrait of transformation reveals the character qualities of the God who is at work in us. These portraits of transformation are not about us. They are all about the God who changes us.

The fact is these portraits of spiritual transformation display incredible character qualities, but they didn't originate from our lives. These qualities come from the Lord Jesus Christ. Therefore, the portraits of transformation in these galleries were never intended to be a hall of fame to honor us for our spiritual achievement. If there is anything in these portraits that is praiseworthy, then the praise goes to God alone! He is the one who imparts these features into our lives.

When someone praises the features of our natural portrait we are immediately proud of our appearance. But when someone praises our features in these spiritual portraits there is no room for pride. We have nothing to do with the wonderful features seen in our portraits of transformation. They are a work of God's grace. All glory and praise go to Him.

Character Qualities

When we see strength in our new likeness, be honest. If it were up to us it wouldn't be there. None of us have the power to cause spiritual transformation. If we see some strength in our portrait, it is because the Holy Spirit is at work. He empowers us. All praise goes to God who keeps on putting into our feeble lives the power of His Holy Spirit!

Maybe our portraits display love. Where is it coming from? Again, it's not from us. Remember we were full of rebellion and selfishness. Love comes from Jesus. It is His great love for the nations that caused Him to come, die, and now intercede for everyone. It is that same love that now flows in our hearts. Jesus Christ is in love with people and He wants to get to them through us. God is pouring into our hearts the love of our Lord Jesus Christ!

Do people see wisdom in our portraits? If so, you can be sure it is not our wisdom. When it comes to spiritual reality we are confused and ignorant. Any wisdom we discover in our portraits is directly from God. He is the one who has figured it all out! And He delights to share with us all we need to know to live for His honor. The only wise God happily invades our minds with His great purposes!

Anything worth admiring in these spiritual portraits is because God is doing a work in us through our faith. If people can't find anything in your spiritual likeness to admire, then you haven't begun to believe for transformation. And if you haven't begun to believe then your tour in these galleries of spiritual portraits is not over. Stay, look and pray until God does something in you through the life-changing person of Jesus Christ.

Before you go, look at Paul's word of praise to God who makes every spiritual transformation in our lives possible. In Romans 16:25–27 he exclaims,

> *"Now to him who is able to establish you by my gospel and the proclamation of Jesus Christ ... so that all the nations might believe and obey him – to the only wise God be glory forever through Jesus Christ! Amen."*

Notes

Chapter 1
1. John K. Ryan, translator, *The Confessions of St. Augustine* (Garden City, New York: Image Book, 1960), pp. 65–67.
2. *Ibid.*, p. 188.
3. *Ibid.*, p. 75.

Chapter 2
4. David Soper, editor, *They Found the Way* (Philadelphia: The Westminister Press, 1961), p. 13
5. *Ibid.*, p. 15.
6. *Ibid.*, p. 23.
7. *Ibid.*, p. 21

Chapter 3
8. A. Skevington Wood, *The Burning Heart* (Minneapolis: Bethany Fellowship Inc., 1967), p. 57.
9. *Ibid.*, p. 57.
10. *Ibid.*, p. 47.

Chapter 4
11. Ryan, *Ibid.*, p. 202.
12. Soper, *Ibid.*, p. 23.
13. Wood, *Ibid.*, p. 59.
14. Soper, *Ibid.*, p. 16.

15. *Ibid.*, p. 25.
16. Wood, *Ibid.*, p. 59.

Chapter 5

17. Thomas C. Upham, *Life and Religious Opinions and Experience of Madame De La Mothe Guyon*, Vol. 1 (New York: Harper and Brothers Publishers, 1874), p. 96.
18. *Ibid.*, p. 97.

Chapter 6

19. Clarence W. Hall, *Samuel Logan Brengle, Portrait of a Prophet* (Chicago: The Salvation Army Supply and Purchasing Dept, 1933), p. 48.
20. *Ibid.*, p. 48.

Chapter 7

21. Agnes Sanford, *Sealed Orders* (Plainfield: Logos International, 1972), p. 217.
22. *Ibid.*, p. 42.
23. *Ibid.*, p. 7.

Chapter 8

24. Hall, *Ibid.*, p. 52.
25. Sanford, *Ibid.*, p. 219.
26. Upham, *Ibid.*, p. 186.
27. Hall, *Ibid.*, p. 49.
28. *Ibid.*, p. 52.
29. Sanford, *Ibid.*, p. 219.
30. Upham, *Ibid.*, p. 185.

Chapter 9

31. A.M. Hill, *Pentecost Rejected and the Effects on the Church* (Cincinnati: Office of God's Revivalist, 1902), p. 14.
32. *Ibid.*, p. 16.
33. *Ibid.*, p. 15.
34. *Ibid.*, p. 21.

Chapter 10

35. Emir Roberts and R. Geraint Gruffydd, *Revival and Its Fruit* (Brynticion, Mid Giamorgan: Evangelical Library of Wales, 1981), p. 24.
36. *Ibid.*, p. 25.
37. *Ibid.*, p. 26.
38. *Ibid.*, p. 35.

Chapter 11

39. James Burnes, *Revival: Their Laws and Leaders* (Grand Rapids: Baker Books, 1960), p. 160.
40. *Ibid.*, p. 124.
41. *Ibid.*, p. 140.
42. *Ibid.*, p. 144.

Chapter 12

43. James Strahan, *The Marechale* (London: James Clarke & Co. Ltd), p. 31–32.
44. *Ibid.*, p. 174.
45. *Ibid.*, p. 175.
46. *Ibid.*, p. 177.

Chapter 13

47. Festo Kivengere, *Revolutionary Love* (Fort Washington: Christian Literature Crusade, 1983), p. 77.
48. *Ibid.*, p. 77.
49. *Ibid.*, p. 80.
50. *Ibid.*, p. 81.

Chapter 14

51. Bruce Olson, *For This Cross I'll Kill You* (Carol Stream: Creation House, 1973), p. 169.
52. *Ibid.*, p. 169.
53. *Ibid.*, p. 169.

Chapter 15

54. Elizabeth Elliot, *A Chance to Die* (Old Tappan, Fleming H. Revell Co., 1987), p. 205.
55. *Ibid.*, p. 181.
56. *Ibid.*, p. 209.

If you have enjoyed this book and would like to help us to send a copy of it and many other titles to needy pastors in the **Third World**, please write for further information or send your gift to:

**Sovereign World Trust
PO Box 777, Tonbridge
Kent TN11 0ZS
United Kingdom**

or to the **'Sovereign World'** distributor in your country.

Visit our website at **www.sovereign-world.org** for a full range of Sovereign World books.